RICH BROTT

BIBLICAL PRINCIPLES FOR

# ACHIEVING PERSONAL SUCCESS

8 CRITICAL INSIGHTS YOU MUST DISCOVER!

Published by
ABC Book Publishing

---

**AbcBookPublishing.com**
Printed in U.S.A.
**Biblical Principles For Achieving Personal Success**
***8 Critical Insights You Must Discover!***

10 Digit ISBN: 1-60185-013-1
13 Digit ISBN (EAN): 978-1-60185-013-3


**First Edition, July 5, 2008**
Richard A. Brott

# About the Author

Rich Brott holds a Bachelor of Science degree in Business and Economics and a Master of Business Administration.

Rich has served in an executive position of some very successful businesses. He has functioned on the board of directors for churches, businesses, and charities and served on a college advisory board. Rich has traveled to more than 25 countries on teaching assignments and business concerns.

Rich Brott has authored 35 books including:

- *5 Simple Keys to Financial Freedom*
- *10 Life-Changing Attitudes That Will Make You a Financial Success*
- *15 Biblical Responsibilities Leading to Financial Wisdom*
- *17 Biblical Principles for Receiving Supernatural Provision*
- *20 Biblical Principles for Understanding the Purpose of Financial Blessing*
- *29 Biblical Principles for Achieving Financial Alignment*
- *30 Biblical Principles for Managing Your Money*
- *35 Keys to Financial Independence*
- *A Biblical Perspective On Giving Generously*
- *A Biblical Perspective On Tithing Faithfully*
- *A Biblical Perspective On Tithing & Giving*
- *Activating Your Personal Faith to Receive*
- *All the Financial Scriptures in the Bible*
- *Basic Principles for Business Success*
- *Basic Principles for Developing Personal and Business Vision*
- *Basic Principles for Managing a Successful Business*

- *Basic Principles for Maximizing Your Personal Cash Flow*
- *Basic Principles for Starting a Successful Business*
- *Basic Principles of Conservative Investing*
- *Biblical Principles for Achieving Personal Success*
- *Biblical Principles for Becoming Debt Free*
- *Biblical Principles for Building a Successful Business*
- *Biblical Principles for Financial Success - Student Workbook*
- *Biblical Principles for Financial Success - Teacher Workbook*
- *Biblical Principles for Personal Evangelism*
- *Biblical Principles for Releasing Financial Provision*
- *Biblical Principles for Staying Out of Debt*
- *Biblical Principles for Success in Personal Finance*
- *Biblical Principles That Create Success Through Productivity*
- *Business, Occupations, Professions & Vocations In the Bible*
- *Family Finance Handbook*
- *Family Finance Student Workbook*
- *Family Finance Teacher Workbook*
- *Public Relations for the Local Church*
- *Successful Time Management*

He and his wife Karen, have been married for 36 years. Rich Brott resides in Portland, Oregon, with his wife, three children, son-in-law and granddaughter.

# Dedication

This book is dedicated to my daughter Jana, whose dream in part, is to serve the needs of the disadvantaged in the area of health care and medicine. Jana is educated, focused, proactive and has engaged her destiny with a passion. Her mother and I are very proud of her accomplishments and look forward to all that God has pre-ordained for her life.

# Table of Contents

# Introduction

You were created with great potential. You have God-given giftings and talents. Sometimes potential is never realized. Realizing your full potential is an ever continuing process of growth. This involves a willingness to try new things, new ways, new ideas.

Dreams worth pursuing do not have to be "big" or "unrealistic." The important thing is living a dream that is really yours. Those who are most fulfilled know what they want and go after it.

Forget the obvious external definitions of success and check the internal or biblical definition of success. Find out what success is in the eyes of God. The Scripture declares, "I can do everything through him who gives me strength. Philippians 4:13 NIV

Ephesians 1:4 says. "According as he hath *chose us* in Him before the foundation of the world, that we should be holy and without blame before Him in love."

You have great God-given capacity to succeed in life! Your life can be full and rewarding. People who never achieve their full potential live an empty life. If you think you can't, you won't. Search for something that can't be done and do it.

***You can achieve the personal success of your dreams!***

*Rich Brott*

# The Principle of Shaping a Personal Vision

# Insight One

# The Principle of Shaping a Personal Vision

*"Where there is no vision, the people perish..."* Proverbs 29:18 (KJV)

*"For I know the plans I have for you," declares the LORD, "plans to prosper you and not to harm you, plans to give you hope and a future."* Jeremiah 29:11 (NIV)

A personal assessment begins with vision. Proverbs 29:18 notes, "Where there is no vision, the people perish..." (KJV) Vision-setting is a collaboration between you and God. Here is an example of that partnership. "In his heart a man plans his course, but the LORD determines his steps." Proverbs 16:9 (NIV)

Proverbs 16:3 "Commit to the LORD whatever you do, and your plans will succeed."

What is it that you are called to do? What is the vision you have for your life? What dreams do you have that are still ahead of you? What were you born to do? What is your purpose? John 18:37 speaks to this issue. "Pilate replied, "But you are a king then?" "Yes," Jesus said. "I was born for that purpose." (TLB)

Ecclesiastes 9:10 encourages you to get started in that pursuit. "Whatever your hand finds to do, do it with all your might, for in the grave, where you are going, there is neither working nor planning nor knowledge nor wisdom." (NIV)

William Jennings Bryan said, "Destiny is not a matter of chance, it is a matter of choice; it is not a thing to be waited for, it is a thing to be achieved."

Vision gives direction. Vision gives motivation. Without vision there is no direction and no motivation. Going through life with no direction is a miserable condition to be in. In your personal life, you need vision. In your family life, you need vision. In business, you need a vision; people do not want to follow someone or something that is without vision.

**Vision Provides:**

- A sense of direction to life
- A sense of discipline to life
- A sense of energy to life

If you don't have a vision for your life, you will end up living an agenda that other people have for you. You will be living out life solely for others and for their vision. You need to have your own vision; your own purpose and calling in life.

Myles Munroe said this, "Perhaps your dreams are so big they almost frighten you. You don't see how they could ever come to pass. Let me assure you that your initial apprehension is normal. God often gives us dreams that confound us at first because He wants to make sure we don't attempt to fulfill them apart from Him. If we try to do so, we won't succeed, because the resources won't be available."[1]

Scripture says that a person's gifting makes room for him (Proverbs 18:16). One translation says it in this way. "A gift opens the way for the giver and ushers him into the presence of the great. " (NIV) What is your gifting? What are the talents that you have within you?

David Clifton observes, "Talents are your naturally recurring patterns of thought, feeling, or behavior. Knowledge consists of the facts and lessons learned. Skills are the steps of activity. These three – talents, knowledge, and skills – combine to create your strengths."[2]

## Shaping Your Personal Vision

**James 4:14-15**

> *Why, you do not even know what will happen tomorrow. What is your life? You are a mist that appears for a little while and then vanishes. Instead, you ought to say, "If it is the Lord's will, we will live and do this or that."*

***What the world offers your personal vision.***

- personal security is not guaranteed
- positions come and go
- jobs disappear
- security in this life is non-existent
- relationships are easily broken
- possessions can be stolen, broken, burnt up, destroyed, lost
- reputations are lost
- good health can fade away
- beauty fades with age
- death can come without advance notice

***What God offers your personal vision.***

- real help
- lasting security
- everlasting life
- behind the scenes assistance
- a life filled with purpose
- a personal vision with a Godly plan

**Esther 4:13-14**

> *For if you remain silent at this time, relief and deliverance for the Jews will arise from another place, but you and your father's family will perish. And who knows but that you have come to royal position for such a time as this?"*

***The biblical character, Esther, had a personal vision.***

- her personal vision was to save her people from extinction
- she risked her own security
- lived a life full of Godly purpose
- a chosen vessel for her time
- risked her future
- her courage did not take the place of careful and strategic planning
- Esther combined purpose, planning and courage
- was open to the advice of others
- was willing to take action
- was more concerned about others than herself
- was a person of great integrity and character
- risked her life for others

- understood that God was working "behind the scenes" to fulfill Esther's personal vision and destiny

***Principles learned from Esther's personal vision.***

- personal vision will guide your life
- personal vision gives you purpose
- God uses others to help you fulfill your destiny
- God will work on your behalf
- God is always working behind the scenes
- move forward with personal purpose even without guarantees of success
- personal vision will always face challenges and setbacks
- our only security is in God and His unchanging nature
- uncomfortable situations and awkward circumstances can actually help us fulfill our personal purpose and vision
- don't be afraid, have faith in God

Is it time to pause for reflection? Stop for a few minutes and write out a sentence or two that captures the following about you. You can call it assessing your potential. It will be your personal analysis, your skill evaluation, and your gifting assessment.

**My Goals**

- *Personal*
- *Family*
- *Religious*
- *Financial*
- *Retirement*
- *Other*

**My Experience**

- *Industry Experience*
- *Job Function Held*
- *Education*
- *Training*
- *Course-work*
- *Other*

**My Skills**

- *Language Skills*
- *Public Speaking*
- *Hobbies*
- *People skills*
- *Financial condition*
- *Other*

**Y** - **Your** personal strengths will be discovered.

**O** - **Obstacles** to personal growth is something you should always be aware of.

**U** - **Use** of your strengths to minimize your weaknesses is important. Anything that would hinder you from reaching your goals and fulfilling your purpose in life must be abandoned.

# The Principle of Understanding Your Full Potential

## Insight Two

# The Principle of Understanding Your Full Potential

You were created with great potential. You have God-given giftings and talents. Sometimes potential is never realized. Realizing your full potential is an ever continuing process of growth. This involves a willingness to try new things, new ways, new ideas.

When it comes to dreams of success, a lot of people have compiled "wish lists." The problem with "wish lists" is that wishing is about as far as many people get in life.

Examples include: I wish I had an education. I wish I had a better job. I wish I had my own business. I wish I could get my pilot's license. I wish...., I wish. Success must always be measured by your purpose in life. This will motivate you, help you set your goals and determine your value system.

Dreams worth pursuing do not have to be "big" or "unrealistic." The important thing is living a dream that is really yours. Those who are most fulfilled know what they want and go after it.

Too often people spend valuable time living out the dream of someone else. For example, if your parents thought that flying an airplane was just too hazardous, chances are you will not leave the interstate highways unless you claim your dream of flying on your own and begin to live out your own personal dreams and visions.

If you are going to take the risk associated with your dreams, start by believing in yourself, your God-given potential and your future. Too many people base their faith in themselves solely on external factors.

Examples include: "If only I had an education; if only I were tall, tan, & handsome; if only I had good relationships in my life; if only I had been born into a family of wealth." If only…if only.

Forget the obvious external definitions of success and check the internal or biblical definition of success. Find out what success is in the eyes of God. The Scripture declares, "I can do everything through him who gives me strength. Philippians 4:13 NIV

Ephesians 1:4 says. "According as he hath chose us in Him before the foundation of the world, that we should be holy and without blame before Him in love."

You have great God-given capacity to succeed in life! Your life can be full and rewarding. People who never achieve their full potential live an empty life. If you think you can't, you won't. Search for something that can't be done and do it.

✓ God has a plan for your life.

> *"For I know the plans I have for you," declares the LORD, "plans to prosper you and not to harm you, plans to give you hope and a future." Jeremiah 29:11 (NIV)*

✓ Most people are unaware of their ability to succeed.

✓ Life is what you make of it.

✓ Get rid of negative thinking

✓ Negative thinking blocks positive action.

✓ Feed your mind with biblical, pure and progressive thoughts, just as you feed your body wholesome food.

✓ Failure is a mindset. Success is a mindset.

✓ Success begins the moment you acquire self-confidence.

✓ You must plan for success.

- ✓ Don't wait for your ship to arrive in port; swim out to meet it.
- ✓ Self-confidence is acquired, not inherited.
- ✓ Create your own opportunities rather than waiting for your "break" in life.
- ✓ Some fail because they lack faith in their own potential.
- ✓ Don't give up! Worthwhile things are often the hardest to achieve.
- ✓ Obstacles are blown apart by perseverance and determination.
- ✓ Negative thinking is self-destructive.
- ✓ Success does not necessarily mean material success. Success includes spiritual peace, emotional maturity, self-respect, and family success.
- ✓ As you achieve success, share your life with others.

God is on your side! He wants you to reach forward into your future and secure the destiny He has for your life.

**Psalms 139:5-6**

*You hem me in — behind and before; you have laid your hand upon me. Such knowledge is too wonderful for me, too lofty for me to attain. (NIV)*

**Romans 8:31**

*"What shall we then say to these things? If God be for us, who can be against us?" (KJV)*

**Psalm 139:13-16**

> *"For you created my inmost being; you knit me together in my mother's womb. I praise you because I am fearfully and wonderfully made; your works are wonderful, I know that full well. My frame was not hidden from you when I was made in the secret place. When I was woven together in the depths of the earth, your eyes saw my unformed body. All the days ordained for me were written in your book before one of them came to be. (NIV)*

Psalms 139 says that God *knew* about you even before you were born. In verse 14 it states that you were fearfully and wonderfully made. In others words, you were created with ***"purpose"***. And according to verse 16, all of your days were ordained for you and written in God's book even before you took your first breath.

Romans 8:28 is one of the best-loved passages in the Bible. It says this. "We know that all things work together for good to them that love God, to them who are the called according to his purpose."

God has a good and great purpose in mind for you. You CAN trust Him with your life.

Christianity deals in *potential*, and what a person can *become*, not what he/she had been in the past or even what they are in the present. This is the very heart of the Gospel.

Find useable qualities, attributes and God-created potential inside that will help you achieve your goals and fulfill your life's purpose. You have a lifetime of potential. Get started!

**P** - Persistence, plan, prioritize
**O** - Obstacles become challenges
**T** - Training…get it; time management….learn it!
**E** - Enthusiasm, energy
**N** - Never give up
**T** - Teach others
**I** - Initiate action, inspire others
**A** - Attitude; get it right
**L** - Learn from others; lead others, be a mentor

Continue your personal assessment and your aptitude for fulfilling your God-given purpose by asking yourself these questions.

| | |
|---|---|
| *Can I weather the storms?* | Keeping a right temperament. Having the right attitude. |
| *Skills, Gifts and Talents:* | Do you know your ability?<br>Do you understand your weaknesses? |
| *Failure:* | Can you accept failure, yet move ahead? |
| *Change Ability:* | Do you learn from your experiences?<br>Can you change and adjust?<br>Do you willingly accept course corrections? |
| *Sacrificial Orientation:* | Can you endure short term pain for long term gain? |
| *Risk Orientation:* | How easily do you accept/manage risk? |
| *Persistence:* | Do you have a "never give up" attitude? |

| | |
|---|---|
| *Learner:* | Do you seek counsel or advice? Can you learn from others? |
| *Visionary:* | Can you hold your vision close until fulfillment? Do you have the ability to sell your vision to others? |
| *Creativity:* | A worthy idea; do you have one? |
| *Detailed:* | Can you perform detailed and thorough research? |
| *Planner:* | A well-thought-out / organized plan; do you have one? |
| *Manager:* | Superb Management. Are you capable? |
| *Wise Decision-Maker:* | Good judgment. Do you have it? |

# The Principle of Envisioning Success

## Insight Three

# The Principle of Envisioning Success

**Joshua 1:8-9**

> *Do not let this Book of the Law depart from your mouth; meditate on it day and night, so that you may be careful to do everything written in it. Then you will be prosperous and successful.*

Becoming prosperous and successful is a direct result of obedience. In this Scripture, God challenges us to meditate upon the Word of God. The emphasis placed here is not upon education, knowledge or experience. It is upon obedience. It is one thing to understand and quite another to walk in obedience.

Study the life of Joshua if you desire success. Some 1300 years before Christ, Joshua was born into a family of Egyptian slavery. Growing up under Egyptian rule he experienced first hand both the plagues of Egypt and the exodus miracle. Arriving at the border of the Promised Land under the great leadership of Moses, he was one of 12 spies that were sent out to scout the land. Only Joshua and Caleb returned with a faith-filled report.

After the death of the prophet Moses, the Lord chose Joshua to get the people ready to cross over into the land of promise. His entire life was one of obedience and faith. When we obey God's provisional principles, He will see to it that we also benefit from biblical principles resulting in prosperity and success.

**Genesis 12:1-3**

*The LORD had said to Abram, "Leave your country, your people and your father's household and go to the land I will show you. "I will make you into a great nation and I will bless you; I will make your name great, and you will be a blessing. I will bless those who bless you, and whoever curses you I will curse; and all peoples on earth will be blessed through you."*

## Abraham envisioned success

- in old age Abraham received a great blessing
- when Abraham was about 70, he moved to Haran with his wife Sarah, nephew Lot and father Terah

**Acts 7:2-3**

*To this he replied: "Brothers and fathers, listen to me! The God of glory appeared to our father Abraham while he was still in Mesopotamia, before he lived in Haran. 'Leave your country and your people,' God said, 'and go to the land I will show you.'*

- separated from his father's house
- left his native land
- he did not know where he was going
- believed that God would lead him to a land of promise

- believed in God's promise that his seed would possess the land
- practiced hospitality always
- he became very rich
- At age 75, Abraham moved again…this time seeking the land of Cannan
- was told that his seed should be as numerous as the stars of heaven (Genesis 15)
- at age ninety-nine his name was changed from Abram to Abraham
- his covenant renewed
- his new name means "father of many people"
- promised a son by Sarah
- visited by angels
- at one hundred years of age, became the father of Isaac
- became founder of the Jewish nation
- was respected by all
- avoided conflict with others when possible
- successfully endured the testing of his faith in God when Isaac was twenty-five years old
- lived a lifetime of unwavering faith
- lived a lifetime of covenant promise

### *Success lessons learned from the life of Abraham*

- even if success is not imminently apparent, speak it in faith
- see your potential as God sees your potential
- age is not a factor in success…you are never too old to start again

- do not discount the blessing of God
- God is pleased by belief and faith in Him
- it is better to avoid conflict with neighbors when possible
- nothing is impossible with God
- God has a plan for your life

## David envisioned success

- David envisioned success when approaching the bear and the lion
- envisioned success when engaging the enemy in battle
- envisioned success when challenging Goliath
- envisioned success when he brought the ark back to Jerusalem
- prepared for success through prayer, fasting and going to battle
- prepared for kingship
- became the greatest and most successful king of Israel

*Success lessons learned from the life of David*

- engage your enemy on their turf
- don't be afraid of the obstacle if God is on your side
- don't let criticism stop your progress
- take action when others hesitate
- meet all challenges head-on
- be willing to admit mistakes
- always to what is right
- let every circumstance teach you something
- prepare for your future by fighting smaller battles now

- befriend those who may be jealous of your success
- learn and grow until it is God's appointed time for you
- ask forgiveness for wrong choices and personal sin
- our worship and trust is desired by God
- trust in God whether you be a shepherd, a poet, a giant-killer, a king or royalty
- trust God whether you be a betrayer, liar, adulterer or murderer
- all actions have consequences
- confessed sin brings forgiveness
- forgiveness brings joy
- perspective makes the difference
- viewing impossible situations from the viewpoint of God, puts giant problems in perspective
- we should look at our challenges from God's point of view
- when others see certain defeat, eyes of faith see victory

**Proverbs 21:17**

> *He who loves pleasure will become poor; whoever loves wine and oil will never be rich.*

This verse tells us that loving pleasure and overindulgence squanders assets and prevents us from building proper financial resources.

Jesus said this in Luke 12:15, "Watch out! Be on your guard against all kinds of greed; a man's life does not consist in the abundance of his possessions."

To live in success and to become successful, you must know what that means to you. Does success differ for dissimilar people, families and cultures? Certainly! In the western world, we live in a culture filled with things and stuff. A life which revolves around things and stuff can be defined as a life filled with materialism. Too often, our spending habits are built upon the foundation of materialism because we want things, and more things. We just can't seem to get enough stuff.

Now hear me out. Having things is not the problem. Having the money to be able to purchase things is not the problem, but *stuff* and *things* should not be bought just because you have the money. Of course, if you don't have the money, they should not even be considered. As biblical stewards, we are not to spend the Master's money on things we don't need. That would be very foolish.

So if having wealth is not the problem, and having possessions is not the problem, then what is the obstacle, the potential stumbling block? The spiritual problem comes with the love of things. When we can't get enough, when we must have more, this is where we stumble spiritually.

But this contradicts many biblical principles. The Christian way is all about servanthood and sacrifice, not materialism and overindulgence.

*One definition of materialism states:*

"The tendency to give undue importance to material interests; devotion to the material nature and its wants." [3]

*Another definition of materialism:*

"A desire for wealth and material possessions with little interest in ethical or spiritual matters." [4]

A. W. Tozer said, "Never own anything; get rid of the sense of possessing!"

"Materialism is a view of life that regards the possession of material things as the highest good, the *summum bonum*. It involves more than a mere appreciation of physical things. It goes beyond the simple enjoyment of material benefits. This view is both radical and an ism. It is radical because it makes material things the heart or 'root' (radix) of all human happiness. It is an ism because it turns the neutral word 'material' into a philosophy of life." [5]

**Luke 12:16-21**

> *And he told them this parable: 'The ground of a certain rich man produced a good crop. He thought to himself, What shall I do? I have no place to store my crops. Then he said, 'This is what I'll do. I will tear down my barns and build bigger ones, and there I will store all my grain and my goods. And I'll say to myself, You have plenty of good things laid up for many years. Take life easy; eat, drink and be merry.' But God said to him, 'You fool! This very night your life will be demanded from you. Then who will get what you have prepared for yourself?' This is how it will be with anyone who stores up things for himself but is not rich toward God.*

Here is a biblical story about a fool and his possessions. He was even called a fool by God! Well, what do YOU think? Was he a fool? Not many people have been so singled out by God. But before you jump on the bandwagon in agreement, read the story again. This story seems to be a picture of the American Dream! The rich man was probably a hard and productive worker. He built and saved and toiled for a lifetime. This is not unlike some people today. They purchase their first little house, and when they outgrow it, they sell it and buy a bigger one. And when they get a little equity in the place, they place it on the market and look for a bigger, better, nicer, newer house!

The man in Luke 12 was shrewd. He was a builder; he was an investor. There is no evidence that he was dishonest, no evidence that he broke the law and no evidence that he evaded paying taxes. None whatsoever. Some people today are just like him. They write best-selling books, give expensive seminars, have university buildings named after them and are proclaimed publicly as entrepreneurs – the individuals that make America great! They work hard, invest well and retire early.

Yet, in Luke 12, Jesus called this man a fool! Why? Is it wrong to be successful? Is it wrong to have wealth? Does this mean that Christians should all be poor? No! Abraham, Isaac, Jacob, Joseph, David, Solomon, Daniel, Joseph of Arimathea and Cornelius were all wealthy. Some of them, in fact, were extremely wealthy.

So what is the difference between the man called a fool by God and these great Old Testament patriarchs and New Testament characters? The difference is this: This man's outlook on life was totally self-centered. Everything he did was for himself. Every event, every purchase, every sale, everything was all about his personal ease and happiness. In his mind, HE, not God, was the sole owner of his life and his possessions. And his priorities – they were so badly skewed that he deserved the tag "fool."

He used his wealth for himself rather than for the kingdom of God. His security was all wrapped up in his ability, his money and his possessions. He was headed for a retirement life of ease, but one without God. A retirement of self-serving gratification, not a retirement of servanthood.

Yes, it's true that the Abrahams, Isaacs, Jacobs, Josephs, Davids, Solomons and Daniels of the Bible were rich. But here is the difference between them and the Luke 12 fool. They had wealth, but each of them was totally devoted to God.

Is it wrong to enjoy the blessing of God? Of course not, but the blessing of God does mean we must have our priorities right in life. First, God must be recognized as the source of all things. Second, He must be credited with full ownership of all we possess. Third, it must be known that our spiritual prosperity is infinitely more important than our material prosperity.

**3 John 2**

*Beloved, I pray that you may prosper in all things and be in health, just as your soul prospers (NKJV)).*

**Proverbs 3:9**

*Honor the LORD with your wealth.*

Many readers of this book would not think their lifestyle is one of wealth and excess. To you the words extravagant and excessive would not seem descriptive of your standard of living. But the reality is that most of you really do live a life of abundance; you travel to where you wish, you buy what you desire and there are very few constraints in your lifetime of opportunities.

Dr. Neil Chadwick explains to us how really wealthy some of us are in the country of my origin (USA) in this excerpt from one of his messages.

*"Recently it has come to my attention just how imbalanced a world we live in. The fact of the matter is, if you have food in the refrigerator, clothes on your back, a roof overhead and a place to sleep, you are richer than 75% of this world. If you have money in the bank, in your wallet, and spare change in a dish someplace - you are among the top 8% of the world's wealthy. If we could shrink the earth's population to a village of precisely 100 people, with all the existing human ratios remaining the same, 6 people would possess 59% of the entire world's wealth and all 6 would be from the United States; 80 would live in substandard housing; 70 would be unable to read; 50 would suffer from malnutrition; and only 1 would have a college education."*

So what do you think about this verse in Proverbs 3:9; "Honor the LORD with your wealth"? Do you think that it applies to someone else? Regardless of whether or not you have great wealth, by the standards of most of the world's citizens, you are a wealthy person.

God has blessed so many with great wealth, assets, and riches compared to just a generation or two ago. What are you doing with your blessing? Are you honoring God or yourself?

**1 Timothy 6:17**

> *Charge them that are rich in this world, that they be not highminded, nor trust in uncertain riches, but in the living God, who giveth us richly all things to enjoy; (KJV)*

Some people have the wrong idea of wealth, relegating it only to $$'s and a huge bank account. But true riches is very different than you might think. Having good health and the ability to enjoy one's family, friends and life in general is what real wealth is all about. God wants us to be happy and enjoy His creation. The following story better demonstrates what this principle is all about.

One day a very rich father took his family on a trip to the country. "How come we're doing this, Dad?" one of the kids wanted to know. "Oh," he replied, "I just want to show you how poor some people can be." So they spent a day and a night at the farm of a very poor family. When they returned from their journey, the father asked his son, "Well, how did you enjoy that?" The young man said, "Aw, it was super, Dad! Thanks!" "And...what did you learn?" the father asked. And his boy answered, "I saw that we have a dog here at home...but that farmer and his family had FOUR dogs." "We have a swimming pool that reaches to the middle of the garden; but they have a creek that doesn't even have an end." "We have imported lamps in our garden; but they have the stars they can see every night." "Our patio reaches to the front yard, but they have a whole horizon."

The boy stopped for a moment and looked at his shaken father. "Dad," he said, "you told me you were going to show me how poor people can be. I get it--we're really poor, aren't we?"

**Malachi 3:10-11**

> *Bring all the tithes into the storehouse so that there will be food enough in my Temple; if you do, I will open up the windows of heaven for you and pour out a blessing so great you won't have room enough to take it in! Try it! Let me prove it to you! Your crops will be large, for I will guard them from insects and plagues. Your grapes won't shrivel away before they ripen," says the Lord Almighty. (TLB)*

Sometimes we don't realize how blessed we are. We think in terms of new cars, clothes, furniture, the size of our house, the size of our bank account, etc. But when this Scripture talks about opening up the windows of heaven and pouring out a great blessing, don't forget all of the wonderful ways in which you have become the recipient of His love and blessing. In this story of a rich landowner and one of his tenant farmers, we see who was the real rich person.

A rich landowner named Carl often rode around his vast estate so he could congratulate himself on his great wealth. One day, while riding around his estate on his favorite horse, he saw Hans, an old tenant farmer. Hans was sitting under a tree when Carl rode by. Hans said, "I was just thanking God for my food." Carl protested, "If that is all I had to eat, I wouldn't feel like giving thanks." Hans replied, "God has given me everything I need, and I am thankful for it."

The old farmer added, "It is strange you should come by today because I had a dream last night. In my dream a voice told me, 'The richest man in the valley will die tonight.' I don't know what it means, but I thought I ought to tell you." Carl snorted, "Dreams are nonsense," and galloped away, but he could not forget Hans' words: "The richest man in the valley will die tonight."

He was obviously the richest man in the valley, so he invited his doctor to his house that evening. Carl told the doctor what Hans had said. After a thorough examination, the doctor told the wealthy landowner, "Carl, you are as strong and healthy as a horse. There is no way you are going to die tonight."

Nevertheless, for assurance, the doctor stayed with Carl, and they played cards through the night. The doctor left the next morning and Carl apologized for becoming so upset over the old man's dream. At about nine o'clock, a messenger arrived at Carl's door. "What is it?" Carl demanded. The messenger explained, "It's about old Hans. He died last night in his sleep."

## Learning to Become Successful

> *"Success is the ability to go from failure to failure with no loss of enthusiasm."*
>
> —Winston Churchill

Everyone wants to succeed. Everyone's definition of success is different. Your motivation is closely linked with your success. Without a success definition, you will not succeed. Success means achieving goals, the process of getting from one point to the next. Success is measured by the accomplishments of your hopes and dreams.

*Write out your personal definition of success.*

- My definition of success is:

______________________________________________________________

______________________________________________________________

______________________________________________________________

______________________________________________________________

**Success is a purpose statement for life; defining, finding and fulfilling that mission.**

Before becoming a successful person there are some things you should be aware of. Here is some good advice from others.

➤ ***Know Yourself:*** Self-delusion or fantasy will insure failure. Before following some pipe-dream, know whether or not you have the personal discipline to follow it through.

➤ ***Be Thorough:*** Many brilliant plans fail due to some minor oversight in the planning process.

➤ ***Be Consistent:*** Many good vision-seeding people with variable temperaments attitudes fail because they do cannot be consistent with others around them.

➤ ***Cutting Loses:*** It does not matter whether the idea is good or bad, or the planning perfect, the successful individual must be able to recognize and deal with an inevitable failure before others do. This is not to say that he/she should not persist in attempts to prove that success can be achieved long after others have fallen by the wayside. But when failure is on its way, he/she must act swiftly.

➤ ***Change Preparation:*** Progress is totally dependent upon change. Changing results from learning experiences, attitudes, skills, market conditions, etc. Success achieved too easily or too early can suggest a degree of infallibility that is nothing but illusion

➤ ***Life's Crossroads:*** There are always seasons in life where one comes to a cross-road. Sometimes it easy to miss one and keep going in the same direction. If you are in business, how much growth do you want? What kind of growth is good or bad? How much control of growth do you have?

There will come a time when one must make a personal assessment. If you are in business, is it time to turn over the business to subordinates more qualified to take it from here. How about the "quality of life" for the entrepreneur? When is it appropriate to spend more time in family activities and recreation than pursuit of new business. How about one's health, etc.

➤ ***Attitude:*** Super-achievers share one characteristic. They take obstacles and failure and convert them into motivators. When you react positively to negative situations, you'll be able to laugh at your troubles.

➤ ***Persistence:*** This is perhaps the most essential quality needed to attain success both in your professional career and in your personal life. If you throw in the towel every time you face adversity, you'll never know how a winner feels. When the going gets rough, stay in the ring and slug it out.

➤ ***Continual Rest:*** Exhaustion and stress are a dangerous combination. Do not let yourself bear the high stress of building personal dreams while at the same time depriving your body the necessary rest and relaxation that it desperately needs. By getting "rest" during the night, you'll be your "best" during the daytime.

➤ ***Exercise:*** Vigorous activity strengthens your body and helps to relieve stress. Medical people insist that people who exercise regularly, age more slowly, remain healthier and feel better than those who do not.

➤ ***Peace:*** Excesses of any kind can be hazardous to your physical and mental health. One must experience peace in body, soul and spirit. Take care of your body, but do not forget to care for your soul and spirit. Your emotional and spiritual health is just as necessary as your physical health.

➤ ***Vision:*** Without a vision, without purpose, no goals can be met. A lack of goals lead to a lack of planning and inaction. Know what your purpose in this life is all about. Set a vision before you. Fill your mind with an image of what can be and what you will accomplish. Let everything in your life revolve around your vision and you'll take on track in spite of varied circumstances. Vision gives focus. Have a vision.

➤ ***Adjust Written Goals:*** Continue to write, rewrite, adjust and re-adjust your goals. Goals and plans often need to be changed to reflect a changing environment.

➤ ***Commit Yourself 100%:*** The successful person doesn't just show up for work, he/she work with intensity, as if their futures depended upon it. And it does! Successful people aren't satisfied with just "good enough." The prize excellence. Be passionate about your work. Take your work to heart. Expect the best from yourself.

➤ ***Know Where You Are Headed:*** The successful person doesn't just show up for work, he/she establishes purpose, goals, plans and then lives by them. Plan do need to be flexible but there is a big difference between have a plan that can be adapted and passively letting other people and circumstances determine your goals.

➤ ***Learn From Experienced People:*** Others have often gone before you. Perhaps it's a related activity or goal, perhaps not. At any rate, most of the same principles for achieving success are good across the board. Learn the principles and be successful in any area you desire!

➤ ***Network With Fellow Climbers:*** There are others in the same race. Yes, the product or service may be different, but the obstacles and barriers are often related. Network, don't go it alone. Find a successful person and be mentored by them.

➤ ***Take The Initiative:*** There is a story told about twelve boys who showed up to answer a help-wanted ad. A broom was partially blocking the hallway, and each boy who went in to be interviewed stepped over the broom on his way to the boss's office. Finally, one boy picked up the broom and moved it to another spot out of the walkway. This was the boy who was hired.

Successful people take the initiative. They do not wait for instructions - they create!

Benjamin Franklin said, "Success doesn't come from making the fewest mistakes — it comes from getting results. You don't get results without action."

## Having an Attitude of Success

*Is a glass of water half-full or half-empty?*

- If you're a pessimist, it's half-empty.
- If your orientation is that of an optimist, it's half-full.
- If you are thirsty enough for opportunity or success, you probably do not even care.

## The Self-Imposed Glass Ceiling

Knowing something CAN be done is half the battle. Without someone telling you just why you cannot do it, you might just go ahead and get it done! In many ways, just thinking that it can be done is the same as knowing it can be done. Now let me tell you a story I heard many years ago.

One young person got a bunch of fleas and put them into a glass jar. A lid was then put on the jar. The fleas began to go crazy jumping all around the jar trying to get out. They jumped so much that it sounded like a small rainstorm as they continued to hit the lid over and over again.

After a few minutes had passed, the fleas continued to jump but no longer hit the bottom of the lid. I guess it must have hurt their little flea heads. The young person than removed the lid from the top of the jar. The fleas were still jumping, but they never jumped out of the jar. They apparently thought they couldn't.

If we think that there is a glass ceiling, we will forever be confined below it. We will stay in the jar forever, even when there is no lid. After you have done your homework, and the go-ahead light appears to be green, don't listen to the naysayers ….step out, step up to your future and get the job done!

**Proverbs 3:10**

> *Then your barns will be filled to overflowing, and your vats will brim over with new wine.*

This is a wonderful promise, the principle of overflowing barns. It is for everyone who meets the condition which precedes the agreement.

*The condition to this guarantee is two-fold.*

1. First, you are to honor God with your possessions.
2. Second, you are to give the first fruits of all of your increase. A great principle which is wrapped by a wonderful promise. Let's see what it all means.

How do we honor the Lord? Today when we honor others we may do so at banquets, special dinners in their honor, we may give them a plaque or special award for their accomplishments or we may honor a friend by sending a card and gift.

Graduates are honored with public recognition and newly weds are honored with a reception. We honor God by making sure that He holds first-place in our lives. We make sure that in the giving of our time, money, trust and prayers, He knows that our hearts are set upon Him. We place Him as Lord of our life by doing so. We honor Him with hearts full of gratitude because of His abundant blessing in our life.

**Proverbs 10:22**

*The blessing of the LORD brings wealth, and he adds no trouble to it.*

Some of the happiest people on earth are those who give generously. On the other hand, some of the most miserable people today are those who cling to every last dime and never use their prosperity to bless others.

**Proverbs 11:25-28**

*The one who blesses others is abundantly blessed; those who help others are helped. Curses on those who drive a hard bargain! Blessings on all who play fair and square! The one who seeks good finds delight; the student of evil becomes evil. A life devoted to things is a dead life, a stump; a God-shaped life is a flourishing tree. (THE MESSAGE)*

## Attributes and Practices of Success

- Compassion: To offer compassion is always one of life's rich experiences.
- Confidentiality: Don't share information you know to be confidential or that you have been asked to keep to yourself.
- Determination: Be persistent, especially when you fail
- Focus on excellence, not perfection.
- Honesty: Always speak and live the truth
- Patience: Whether you're eager to speak next or to reach your next goal, accept that "your turn will come." This doesn't mean settling for inaction, however. Being patient isn't the same as being complacent
- Punctuality: Be on time, every time
- Purity: Reject anything that lowers your personal standards or the standards of those you serve
- Responsibility: Be trustworthy and dependable
- Self-control: Make wise decisions. Don't let emotion lead you astray or let a fear of being wrong hold you back from making decisions
- Set clear objectives and milestones to check your progress toward your goals.
- Thoughtfulness: Think of others before yourself

# Maximizing Your Success

If you would like to maximize the possibility of moving into the area of success in your personal life, consider these points.

- ✓ Accept Responsibility For Your Success
- ✓ Allow time for relaxation
- ✓ Avoid over-commitment
- ✓ Avoid problems
- ✓ Be Flexible
- ✓ Be Flexible To Obstacles
- ✓ Be Persistence
- ✓ Be quick to find solutions
- ✓ Change As Necessary
- ✓ Concentrate On Your Priorities
- ✓ Coordinate activities
- ✓ Encourage others & yourself
- ✓ Focus on results
- ✓ Get more important things done
- ✓ Keep people focused
- ✓ Know Your Passion, Purpose
- ✓ Manage staff
- ✓ Minimize Interruptions That Take Away Your Focus
- ✓ Persistence
- ✓ Promote a team environment
- ✓ Review Written Goals
- ✓ Review Your Progress
- ✓ Say no more often
- ✓ Seek Help
- ✓ Share information with others
- ✓ Streamline work flow
- ✓ Surround Yourself With Winners
- ✓ Think ahead

✓ When You Reach One Goal, Cross It Off Your List And Get Going On The Next One

## Six Important Keys to Success

1. Capitalizing on Opportunity
2. Commitment
3. Desire
4. Intelligence / Experience
5. Minimizing Pitfalls
6. Positive Attitude

> *"People inhabit this earth by the billions. Flocks increase, plants grow. When I was younger there was much talk about a population explosion and prediction of famine, or scarcity. Food was to run out, the life as we know it was to end. But things kept getting better. Technology lets fewer farmers produce more food. New discoveries of oil and gas occur. Whole industries which did not exist in the 50s and 60s now employ millions. There simply is no credible law of scarcity. We have abundance in this earth. Computer chips from sand, service industries, information and processing ideas, as in the communication arena. It is the opposite of the predictions."*[6]

## Attitudes of Success

Success is an attitude and our attitude makes all the difference in a productive life. Most of altitude is controlled by your attitude.

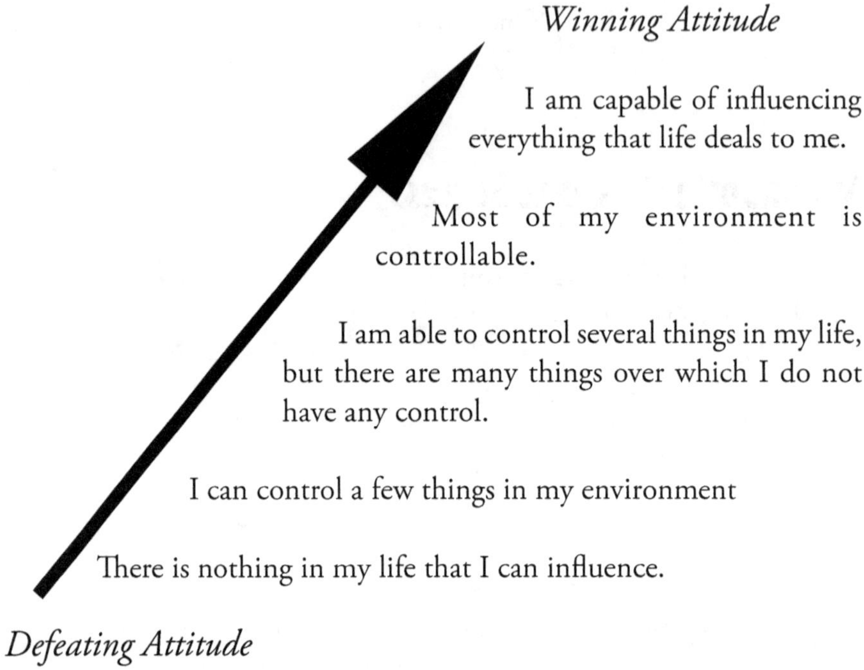

*Winning Attitude*

I am capable of influencing everything that life deals to me.

Most of my environment is controllable.

I am able to control several things in my life, but there are many things over which I do not have any control.

I can control a few things in my environment

There is nothing in my life that I can influence.

*Defeating Attitude*

> *"While it is possible for people with great talent or drive to achieve with a bad attitude, it doesn't happen very often, and it takes an incredible amount of effort. And even if they do achieve some degree of success, they aren't happy. Most often, people with bad attitudes don't get very far in life."*[7]

***A winning attitude helps you to:***

- Break out of your box that restricts inspiration, and limits your potential
- Break Your Bad Habits
- Breakdown Barriers To Creativity

- Embrace New Perspectives
- Forget your traditional perspective and approach change from other viewpoints.
- Practice Creativity
- Think In Positives And Potential
- Try new ideas, new solutions to problems, new ways of doing things, etc.
- Try Out New Ways And Ideas
- View Failures As Opportunities

## Success

*The road to success is always under construction.*

*Success comes in cans.*
*Failure comes in can'ts.*

*To succeed, it is necessary to accept the world as it is and rise above it.*

*Obstacles are things you see when you take your eyes off the goal.*

# The Principle of Personal Diligence

## Insight Four

# The Principle of Personal Diligence

**Proverbs 21:25, 26**

*The sluggard's craving will be the death of him, because his hands refuse to work. All day long he craves for more, but the righteous give without sparing.*

**Romans 12:11**

*Not slothful in business; fervent in spirit; serving the Lord. KJV*

**Proverbs 24:30-34**

*I went past the field of the sluggard, past the vineyard of the man who lacks judgment; thorns had come up everywhere, the ground was covered with weeds, and the stone wall was in ruins. I applied my heart to what I observed and learned a lesson from what I saw: A little sleep, a little slumber,a little folding of the hands to rest – and poverty will come on you like a bandit and scarcity like an armed man.*

It is everyone's responsibility to be hard working, persistent, and diligent. The person who has no diligence is lazy – a sluggard, if you will.

The sluggard. What can be said about this kind of person? Is he self-centered or lazy? Does he rest; does he do what he wants to do without regard to others? Certainly all these things probably describe a sluggard, but much more could be said.

At the very least, a sluggard has a major problem with procrastination. His motto would be to "never do today what you can put off until tomorrow"; always with good intentions; always just about ready to start a job, but not quite.

The sluggard probably gets started on a few jobs, and with some of those tasks he may even get some things done, but never quite gets them finished or brought to completion.

What is his excuse? Maybe he didn't have all the tools to finish the job. Maybe he wasn't feeling well. Maybe the rain was on its way or it could be just that the sun was not shining brightly enough.

Perhaps his excuse is that the job became bigger than he was expecting or it became more time consuming than he was willing to commit to. Whatever the excuse, the sluggard always finds a reason for not finishing the job.

Matthew 3:12 says, "He is ready to separate the chaff from the grain with his winnowing fork. Then he will clean up the threshing area, storing the grain in his barn but burning the chaff with never-ending fire." (NLT)

"When harvesting wheat, the job is not complete until the grain is in the barn and the threshing floor is clean. Only then can the farmer take satisfaction in a job well done."[8]

The sluggard as portrayed in Proverbs is an example of what not to be like and presents a valuable lesson for us to learn. Proverbs 20:4 tells us that the sluggard is too lazy to pull a plow in the springtime, and therefore has no harvest in the fall. In Proverbs 22:13, he lets his mind wander, but refuses to move his body. He has a great reason why he can't get it into gear.

He says there could be a lion outside, and if he goes out to work, he could be murdered in the streets! Whatever the situation, when the sluggard makes up his mind that he doesn't feel like working today, he will find an excuse to justify his inaction. He will find some kind of plausible explanation for his decision. He will leap to shirk his responsibilities, for he has a quick mind and a lazy body.

The ancient Chinese philosopher Confucius once said, "The expectations of life depend upon diligence; the mechanic that would perfect his work must first sharpen his tools."

Samuel Johnson noted, "If your determination is fixed, I do not counsel you to despair. Few things are impossible to diligence and skill. Great works are performed not by strength, but perseverance."

William Penn equates faith and diligence when he said, "Patience and diligence, like faith, remove mountains."

Proverbs 12:27 says, "The lazy man does not roast his game, but the diligent man prizes his possessions."

Here is the picture of a sluggard who is not only lazy, but also wasteful. Not only does he do what he wants to, when he wants to, but he is also is a great waster of resources and provision. He goes out, he hunts his game, he kills his game. But after the fun of the hunt, the work never begins. He could prepare the provision for his family or the poor, the needy and the hungry, but he instead chooses to walk away from it, lets it die and lie and does not make the food available for the hungry.

Diligent people don't waste God's provision. They thank God for the provision and prepare the meat for future use. They share it with others. They continue diligently using the resources available to them.

Sluggards are not like that. They are not interested in saving resources and helping others. To them it is all about the fun of the sport. They are wasteful about everything. Sluggards proclaim that when their ships come in, they will begin to give. Herein lies the problem: If you never sent your ship out to begin with, you cannot expect it to come in. For what kind of ship are you waiting? Money does not fall from heaven. God does not give money miracles to a lazy, slothful person.

If you are not going to live the life of a sluggard, you need to get your act together. You need to start working, using godly wisdom and insight. You need to understand your calling and purpose in life and set out objectives that will allow you to live that fulfilled life. Then, and only then, will you reap with joy what you have sowed with tears.

> *"Plans fail for lack of counsel, but with many advisers they succeed" Proverbs 15:22.*

Success is always the result of a lot of planning, intense work, good habits and continual follow through. We are what we repeatedly do. Excellence is not an act but a habit. In fact the only place that you will find success before work is in the dictionary.

Success is a planned event and rarely happens without great personal effort. God can bless our productivity, but cannot bless the habits of a lazy person. Success comes in cans. Failure comes in cannots.

Philippians 4:13 says, "I can do all things through Christ who strengthens me (NKJV).

Another great Scripture which talks about blessing those who are productive is found in 2 Corinthians 9:8-10. "And God is able to provide you with every blessing in abundance, so that you may always have enough of everything and may provide in abundance for every good work. As it is written, "He scatters abroad, he gives to the poor; his righteousness endures for ever." He who supplies seed to the sower and bread for food will supply and multiply your resources and increase the harvest of your righteousness." (RSV)

## Implementing Productivity

Good stewardship is not merely an occupation or a profession, rather it involves being productive. In Jesus' parable of the talents in Matthew 25, the stewards reported their earnings. One servant, however, merely hid his entrustment, and earned no increase – he lost his portion.

The faithful ones not only had increases but also, received more because of their faithfulness. From the very beginning, God commanded creation to be fruitful. God is energetic, creative and imaginative, and is the life giver. Stewards or managers are to be concerned with productivity and so cultivate God's creation to be productive.

It is a privilege to live in a productive society. Productive societies are composed of many productive individuals. When my days are full of productive tasks I enjoy life. My normal going-to-sleep activity is to close my eyes and mentally survey all the productive things I accomplished during the day. If I have had an efficient and industrious day, I fall quickly to sleep.

A warning about being productive is seen in Jesus' story about the unfruitful branch of His kingdom, which He says will be cut off by the husbandman (John 15:1-5). God wants to have a productive Kingdom and stewards who will be faithful.

As good stewards, we are required to work hard. If you work for someone else, you need to do it with everything you have. Give more than is required; go the second mile and the third and fourth.

Proverbs 6:6-11 says, "Go to the ant, you sluggard; consider its ways and be wise! It has no commander, no overseer or ruler, yet it stores its provisions in summer and gathers its food at harvest. How long will you lie there, you sluggard? When will you get up from your sleep? A little sleep, a little slumber, a little folding of the hands to rest and poverty will come on you like a bandit and scarcity like an armed man."

Check out the ant. The ant has no one to tell it what to do – no supervisor, nor overseer, and yet it is a self-starter, a self-motivator. The ant works all summer long gathering food for the harvest season.

The Scripture extends a wake-up call to the sluggard hoping for some kind of response. It says to the sluggard, "Have you not slept enough?" "How long can you possibly sleep?" "Do you want to go hungry, do you want to go through life looking for handouts because you have not the wherewithal to earn your own keep?"

## Scriptures on Productivity

**Matthew 17:27**

> *"...go to the lake and throw out your line. Take the first fish you catch; open its mouth..."*

We are to take action—to be proactive. The abilities and giftings that He provides motivate us to action. Sometimes it takes our persistence in doing the same things faithfully with the heart of a servant. Other times, it is useful to try new things or new methods and seek after new opportunities. Sometimes it is the steady plodding that brings the success of the blessed life.

Ecclesiastes 9:11 says, "The race is not to the swift or the battle to the strong, nor does food come to the wise or wealth to the brilliant or favor to the learned; but time and chance happen to them all" .

Hebrews 12:1-2 advises, "…let us throw off everything that hinders and the sin that so easily entangles, and let us run with perseverance the race marked out for us. Let us fix our eyes on Jesus, the author and perfecter of our faith…".

Proverbs 21:5 instructs us that, "Steady plodding brings prosperity; hasty speculation brings poverty" (TLB).

Taking action, being proactive, and not giving up are principles for living the life of a successful and blessed person. Nothing will be thrown into our laps. No, prosperity is not an unconditional providential blessing, and yes, conditions are attached. We are to take action and be proactive.

The abilities and giftings God provides for us as individuals should motivate us to action. Sometimes it takes our persistence in doing the same things faithfully with the heart of a servant. Other times, it is time to try new things, new methods and seek new opportunities. Sometimes it is simply the steady plodding that brings success to your personal world.

*This verse tells us what to do and what to avoid:* "Let us throw off everything that hinders and the sin that so easily entangles, and let us run with perseverance the race marked out for us. Let us fix our eyes on Jesus, the author and perfecter of our faith." Hebrews 12:1, 2

Building success on principle requires hard work, diligence and proactivity. Nothing will be handed to you without these requirements. The Bible says that if a person does not work, he should not eat. Now that's a pretty simple yet direct statement. Does God want to bless your personal life, your professional life and your business life? Of course, He does. Will His blessing come to us if we are lazy, idle, slothful, passive and unwilling to roll up our sleeves and get to work? No, I don't believe so.

**Proverbs 21:25, 26**

*The sluggard's craving will be the death of him, because his hands refuse to work. All day long he craves for more, but the righteous give without sparing.*

*Taking action, being proactive, not giving up – all are principled requirements that create and build successful people.*

**1 Thessalonians 4:11**

*Make it your ambition to lead a quiet life, to mind your own business and to work with your hands, just as we told you, so that your daily life may win the respect of outsiders and so that you will not be dependent on anybody.*

**Proverbs 22:29**

*Do you see a man skilled in his work? He will serve before kings; he will not serve before obscure men.*

**Ecclesiastes 9:10**

*Whatever your hand finds to do, do it with all your might.*

**Proverbs 20:4**

*A sluggard does not plow in season; so at harvest time he looks but finds nothing.*

According to the above scriptures, we should approach life and work like the ant. Although the ant has no boss, it still works extremely hard to provide for its needs. A lot of people today could learn a valuable lesson from the ant. Some today have the attitude that if I can get someone else to do the work for me, then why should I exert myself.

Why not let someone else do the work; why not let the government provide for me? Many today have little or no initiative, are not able to put themselves to work, and must always have someone else instruct them and supervise them in order to keep them working. The biblical way is for each person to accept the personal responsibility to be a contributor to society and a person of productivity.

# The Principle of Forming Good Habits

## Insight Five

# The Principle of Forming Good Habits

Success can be made or broken by the habits you form. Our habits have great influence upon our success in life. Habits can be major obstacles to becoming successful. Habits can be the foundation of your successes. Most everything you do is the result of habits. All habits are learned…and that is good news!

We first form habits; then habits form us! On our road to success, if we do not consciously form good habits, we will unconsciously form bad ones. So we form habits both unconsciously or consciously.

Habits are not instincts; they are acquired reactions. They don't "just happen," they are caused. What we continue to do over and over again becomes a habit. Our lives become the sum total of our habits. Once you have determined the original cause of a habit, it is within your power either to accept or to reject it.

Every person who is successful has simply formed the habits of doing things that failures dislike doing and will not do. It is just as easy to form the habit of succeeding as it is to succumb to the habit of failure.

The harvest we reap in our lives is measured by the attitudes and habits we cultivate. Our habits can be the basis for success or the basic for failure. As such they can predict the future. What you are doing now is what will determine your future.

Your behavior is based on the accumulation of all your experiences. Most of your actions and reactions are automatic, unconscious responses to the habits you have formulated over the years.

Bad habits can become major roadblocks to your success. Between the "where you are today" and the "where you want to be tomorrow" often stands the "habits you are bound by today."

Your habits keep you "running in place." In the absence of some outside influence, or a personal decision on your part to do something different, your habits will keep you doing, reacting, and being the same as you've always been.

When habits become major obstacles to your happiness or performance, they must be discarded completed or modified to bring them into line with your life. Bad habits include being late for appointments or late in completing assignments. Successful people are always punctual and dependable. Successful people respect the time of others and keep their commitments.

Proverbs 23:7 had this to say about our habits of thought. "For as he thinks in his heart, so is he". (NKJV) Bad thought patterns and habits can be very detrimental to your success. Whatever you think about continually, you will create in your life.

Negative, self-limiting thoughts hurt you more than almost anything else. You live in a mental world. Nothing physical around you has much meaning except the meaning you give it with your thoughts. If you can change your way of thinking, you can change your results.

Habits are only good as long as they serve your purpose. Good habits should continually enrich and improve your life. Success and failure, happiness and unhappiness are largely the result of habit. A good life is the result of automatic ways you respond and react to what's going on around you.

Habits that are no longer consistent with your life purposes must be changed. Changing bad habits is essential to the quality of your life. Unless you have already reached some level of excellence or perfection, you are "right now", "today," living with one or more (maybe one hundred or more) habits that should be discarded.

Bad habits are easy to form. Many just form automatically by default. Bad habits are hard to live with.

Good habits are hard to form. They never form automatically. Good habits are easy to live with. Your #1 priority should be to form good, purpose-fulfilling, goal-reaching habits. Don't be controlled by bad habits. Make good habits your master.

A very insightful proverb whose author is unknown, follows.

***Plant a thought, harvest an act.***
***Plant an act, harvest a habit.***
***Plant a habit, harvest a character.***
***Plant a character, harvest a destiny.***

What about your regular habits. Do they lead to the blessing of God? Can God supernaturally provide for you based on your habitual acts? Are they principled, ethical and biblically based?

Habits are often the basis for success or failure. Although people form many habits, both good and bad, habits are the basis for the future. You can form habits unconsciously or consciously. On our road to success, if we do not consciously form good habits, we will unconsciously form bad ones.

Every person who is successful has simply formed the habits of doing things that God can bless. Success and failure, happiness and unhappiness are largely the result of habit.

The attitudes and habits we cultivate, measure the harvest we reap in our lives. Blessed people can be found everywhere. Successful people are everywhere. They are not extraordinary people, although many have lived extraordinary lives. All have particular qualities in common. These are not qualities you inherit, rather you must develop them through education and through hard work.

It's not what happens to you that counts as much as how you react to what happens. All blessed people pattern their personal and work lives after biblical principles, are productive and efficient in business and actively seek the supernatural provision of God.

## Achievers of Personal Success

- The have a predisposition for action; they get the job done.
- They accept 100% of the responsibility for results.
- They are courageous and risk takers.
- They are spiritually aligned.
- They are functionally focused; they know where they are going and how to get it done.
- They are highly decisive; they move things forward continuously.
- They are impeccably honest.
- They are inquisitive; they don't get lazy mentally.
- They are intensely goal-oriented.
- They are persistent and committed.
- They have a sense of urgency; they get more done, and on time.
- They have above average ambition.
- They have above-average will power.
- They have purpose; and seek to fulfill it.
- They have tremendous desire; they look at the reward not the challenge.
- They welcome evaluation and assessment.

## Successful Productive People

*What would be the typical job description of a successful person?*

The successful person is always in the process of bringing his/her "vision / purpose" into reality. This process can best be compared to a juggler spinning a series of plates on tall narrow poles. As a new plate is set spinning the juggler must return to those plates he started earlier in order to keep up their momentum.

The action becomes furious as more plates are spun, and the danger of one or more falling from its pole increases. Like the juggler, the successful person sees the end state of all the plates spinning in perfect timing and sequence as his personal vision. His energies are spent on keeping all the components working toward that common goal.

*The successful person can be described in this manner:*

- His/ her chosen career is lonely.
- No one seems to understand their work load; or even can understand.
- There is no typical day or week.
- Requires 24 hour / 7 day availability.
- The path is filled with risk.
- Day is maximized with difficulty.
- Potential failure is always there.
- The capacity for mistakes is widespread.
- He/she is disparaged for failing.
- He/she may be disliked for eventual success.
- The path is always exhausting physically, mentally and emotionally.
- Acceptance of responsibility
- Capacity for hard work
- Desire to achieve
- Drive to complete projects
- Nurturing quality
- Optimism
- Organizational ability

- Orientation to excellence
- Reward orientation

*Here are some things to watch as you build your dreams.*

- Accept Responsibility
- Attitude – Great people share one characteristic. They take obstacles and failure and convert them into motivators.
- Be Flexible To Obstacles
- Be Persistent.
- Break Your Habits. Ask yourself, "Is there another way to accomplish this?"
- Breakdown Barriers To Creativity. Find the barriers to developing and implementing new ideas and remove them. Old barriers such as, "It won't work any other way; it's against policy; people won't embrace it; it's against operating procedures" just don't fit in today's management culture.
- Change As Necessary.
- Compassion. To offer compassion is always one of life's rich experiences.
- Concentrate On Your Priorities.
- Confidentiality. Don't share information you know to be confidential or that you have been asked to keep to yourself.
- Determination. Be persistent, especially when you fail.
- Develop a learning process. Failure isn't failure as long as we learn from it.
- Effort. The only way to get something you want is to put in the effort required to get it. There are no easy answers, no get-rich-quick schemes, just plenty of scams which will only serve to derail you from your potential success.

- Embrace New Perspectives. Forget your traditional perspective and approach change from other viewpoints.
- Exercise. Vigorous activity strengthens your body and helps to relieve stress. Medical experts insist that people who exercise regularly, age more slowly, remain healthier and feel better than those who do not.
- Giving back to others. The most treasured aspect of being successful is that it enables you to help others achieve the same.
- Honesty. Always speak and live the truth.
- Mentors. Learn to ask for help and support, and find resources for getting the help you need.
- Minimize Interruptions That Take Away Your Focus.
- Passionate pursuit. Seek the favor of God with passion.
- Patience. Whether you're eager to speak next or to reach your next goal, accept that "your turn will come." This doesn't mean settling for inaction, however. Being patient isn't the same as being complacent.
- Peace. Excesses of any kind can be hazardous to your physical and mental health. One must experience peace in body, soul and spirit. Take care of your body, but do not forget to care for your soul and spirit. Your emotional and spiritual health are just as necessary as your physical health.
- This is perhaps the most essential quality needed to attain success both in your professional career and in your personal life. If you throw in the towel every time you face adversity, you'll never know how a winner feels. When the going gets rough, stay in the ring and slug it out.
- Practice Creativity. Try new ideas, new solutions to problems, new ways of doing things, etc.
- **Punctuality**. Be on time, every time, every meeting, every deadline, every part of your life.

- **Purity**. Reject anything that lowers your personal standards or the standards of those you serve.
- **Responsibility**. Be trustworthy and dependable.
- **Rest.** Exhaustion and stress are a dangerous combination. Do not let yourself bear the high stress of building personal dreams while at the same time depriving your body the necessary rest and relaxation that it desperately needs. By getting "rest" during the night, you'll be your "best" during the daytime.
- **Review Your Progress.**
- **Seek Help.**
- **Self-control**. Make wise decisions. Don't let emotion lead you astray or let a fear of being wrong hold you back from making decisions.
- **Setting goals.** Blessed people turn passion into practical reality.
- **Think In Positives And Potential.** Negative thinking inhibits growth and potential.
- **Thoughtfulness**. Think of others before yourself.
- **Try Out New Ways And Ideas.** Don't accept, "It won't work any other way" until you've tried alternative solutions.
- **View Failures As Opportunities.** One of the most common aspects of success is the ability and the willingness to accept the challenges failure presents.
- **Vision achievement.** Without a vision, without purpose, no goals can be met. A lack of goals leads to a lack of planning and inaction. Know what your purpose in this life is all about. Set a vision before you.

Fill your mind with an image of what can be and what you will accomplish. Let everything in your life revolve around your vision and you'll take on track in spite of varied circumstances. Vision gives focus. Have a vision!

# The Principle of Managing Your Time

## Insight Six

# The Principle of Managing Your Time

I will be taking considerable time and writing much on this timely topic. If you cannot discipline yourself to use your time efficiently and productively you will never be a successful person. Time is a very valuable commodity. God blesses individual effort.

Achieving personal success requires efficient and productive use of our time. We are required to redeem the minutes and capture the hours. We should be filling efficient days and occupying industrious weeks. Our effective and productive months should result in productive years. We have a responsibility not to waste the precious little time we have been given.

Several years ago, I traveled to a small town with a couple of friends. Our mission was to paint the house of a dying man. The house was in need of a fresh coat of paint and we were wanting to pay him a visit. Instead of just standing around watching his pain, we intended to help brighten his day by painting the house.

As we were saying our good-byes at the end of the day, he made a profound statement I still remember as if it were yesterday. He said, "It pays to give it all you've got while you're on stage, because you never know when your act is up." Soon afterward, he died of cancer. And since that event I have lost many close friends to various illnesses. I often have wondered, why them and not me? Some of the finest Christians I have known, have been taken pre-maturely. While we certainly do not have the answers to tough situations, we do know that time is a heavenly endowment.

Time is our tool. It is a wonderful gift. We should not be a slave to it; we should put it to proper use as an investment for the future.

God is the giver of life and the giver of time. He has the right to expect us to use it wisely. We have a responsibility to make the most of it. Good stewards of time and finance are not only faithful and responsible, but also have an honesty and financial integrity about them.

God is the God of the past, present and future. He has no time constraints. He is not bound by the limitations of time. Time means nothing to Him. See what the Word says about it.

**2 Peter 3:8**

*But do not forget this one thing, dear friends: With the Lord a day is like a thousand years, and a thousand years are like a day.*

On earth, we (you and I) are constrained by time. Our lives are but a few years, at best. Our time is limited. Time means a lot to us. God has allotted us just a limited amount of years and, therefore, is very concerned how wisely we spend those years.

**Job 14:1, 2**

*"Man born of woman is of few days and full of trouble. He springs up like a flower and withers away; like a fleeting shadow, he does not endure."*

**Psalm 90:10**

*The length of our days is seventy years — or eighty, if we have the strength; yet their span is but trouble and sorrow, for they quickly pass, and we fly away.*

**Ephesians 5:15, 16**

> *Be very careful, then, how you live — not as unwise but as wise, making the most of every opportunity, because the days are evil.*

**John 9:4, 5**

> *As long as it is day, we must do the work of him who sent me. Night is coming, when no one can work. While I am in the world, I am the light of the world.*

Time is valuable and utterly irretrievable; it is a priceless commodity. Suppose your bank credited your account each morning with $86,400.00, carried no balance from day to day, and allowed you to keep no cash in your account. Then suppose every evening the bank canceled whatever you failed to use during the day.

We all have this kind of bank; its name is time. Every morning it credits us with 86,400 seconds. Every night it considers lost whatever time we have failed to invest for good during the day. It carries over no balance. It allows no overdrafts. Each day it opens up a new account. Each night it burns the records of the day. If you failed to use the day's deposits, the loss is yours.

We are all given 1,440 minutes each day, 168 hours each week. This makes 52 weeks each year for which we must account. In spite of its value and unique characteristics, we probably waste time more thoughtlessly than anything else.

Adlai Stevenson once said, "It's not the days in your life, but the life in your days." In other words, it's not how much you do that counts, it's how much you get done that has purpose and lasting benefit.

This seems to be the great paradox in life. We generally feel as though we don't have enough time, yet we have all the time there is. Time is NOT the problem; the problem is how we use our allotted time.

"It matters to God how we use our time. Our affairs are His affairs. It doesn't mean we are slaves to unpleasant obligations. Even Jesus rested and went to places apparently for enjoyment."[9]

***Some facts about time:***

- ✓ Time is our tool. It is a wonderful gift. We should not be a slave to it; but we should put it to proper use as an investment for the future
- ✓ Most of us would never think of going through life without budgeting and investing our finances. Yet, most of us waste a great percentage of our time. It is just as important to study the stewardship of time as it is to study the stewardship of our finances.
- ✓ Money can be spent, or it can be invested. The same is true of time. To invest either is to use them in such a way as to bring future benefits.
- ✓ The benefits of investing time are often realized later in time – usually when time has become a scarce commodity. Time carefully planned and invested will rarely be wasted.
- ✓ People sometimes say that "time passes." But in reality it does not. We go by. Time stands still. Time does not help a person to help themselves. It is how we use the time that is allotted to us that really counts.
- ✓ In time management, all roads lead to the management of self. Often we say, "I wish I could manage my time better." What we should really be saying is, "I wish that I could manage myself better!" The management of our time and ourselves takes perseverance and self-discipline, but no investment pays higher dividends.

# Achieving Means Managing Yourself & Managing Your Time

Self Management is another word for time management. Everyone wants more time. Give time to some people and it's like giving too much candy to a small child....they get into trouble real fast and it can become a disaster. For others, more time or better time management becomes a great asset to them and their business.

***Note the following guidelines with respect to the management of one's self and time.***

- If you do not respect your time, no one else will.
- Everyone has the same amount of time. Some use it wisely, others waste this precious resource.
- Using time is a matter of choice. Some choose to use it wisely and accomplish great things. They invest in their pre-planned goals and objectives. Other choose to invest their time in areas of minimal return.
- You can work hard or work smart. Actually, you should first work smart, and then work hard. While working hard can be an admirable quality, it is not enough. Working smart is knowing what to do and what not to do. It's fairly easy to know which ideas/projects need your attention, but it is harder to know which ones you should not be spending time with.
- Beginning each day with reflection and answering the question, "What do I want to accomplish today, instead of what do I need to get done today" is not only wise but imperative. There is an "attitudinal" difference in the two questions. The first question is proactive and the second is reactive. With the first, you attack your day. With the second, your day attacks you. Who's running whom? Are you calling the shots, or is the day running you? Do you run your life or does your life run you?

# Achieving Means Controlling Your Life

***Consider these observations.***

- Not having control of your life can cause you to have a negative outlook on your environment and yourself.
- Having control of your life can cause you to have a positive outlook on your environment and yourself.
- The degree to which you feel you have some control in life usually is the degree to which you feel positive or negative about your future.
- Control begins with your thoughts. You can have complete control over this area. How you think about your circumstances or any given situation determines how you feel. How you feel determines your behavior. Self-discipline, self-control and self-management all begin with taking control of your thinking and thought life. Eleanor Roosevelt once said, "No one can make you feel inferior without your consent."
- Different seasons in our lives, some circumstances and certainly many situations we find ourselves involved in, can cause us a lot of stress and unhappiness. When you find yourself in unpleasant environments, you can take some action. First of all, you can move forward and do something to change it. You can take hold of the situation and make it different somehow. Secondly, you can simply walk away from it. Sometimes you regain control by letting go of the person or situation and by getting busy reaching toward something else; another goal, another project, another customer, etc.
- Keeping in control is the result of good choices and wise decisions. This is why it is so important to know your purpose in life, the goals you wish to achieve and having a plan of action

for reaching those goals. You must know what it is exactly that you want out of life; and how you will serve your purpose. One of your main responsibilities in life is to get control of it. This sense of control becomes your foundation for building greater happiness and success in the future. Be sure of your purpose. Make sure it's rock solid.

## Achieving by Choosing Between Commitments

A great part of self management is choosing correctly between commitments. More important is choosing what to commitment to and what to set aside. Where are you going to spend your precious time?

***Here are some serious questions to consider.***

✓Is This Important?

✓Does It Focus On My Purpose?

✓Will It Help Achieve One Of My Goals?

✓Is It An Immediate Priority?

✓Why Is This Important?

✓Why Should I Get Involved?

✓Is Now The Proper Time?

## Achieving by Making a "To Do" List

One of the most effective self management tools are "TO DO" lists. I use several of them, depending upon the general category that I need a list for.

***Here is why they are so effective.***

- They create a systematic framework.
- Your day becomes organized.
- Deadlines that are crucial can be met.
- It can be a designation to others what is most important.
- It enables you to be very productive.
- It helps you resist unimportant interruptions.
- High-priority tasks get done first.
- Your personal or internal communication is put to paper.
- Your mind is always clear on what must be done.
- It helps you pace your time better.
- Procrastination is avoided.
- Productive hours are within your grasp.
- Significant progress can be made without being a workaholic.
- Start to finish - the day can be logical.
- Unnecessary worry is brought to a halt.
- You can take it with you during the day.

## TAKE SOME TIME TO:

Time management requires that you appropriately balance your obligations. Schedule in important personal time.

**TAKE TIME TO WORK**
— it is the price of success.

**TAKE TIME TO THINK**
— it is the source of power.

**TAKE TIME TO PLAY**
— it is the secret of youth.

**TAKE TIME TO READ**
— it is the foundation of knowledge.

**TAKE TIME TO ENJOY FRIENDS**
— it is the source of happiness.

**TAKE TIME TO DREAM**
— it hitches the soul to the stars.

**TAKE TIME TO LAUGH**
— it is the singing that helps with life's loads.

**TAKE TIME TO PLAN**
— it is the secret to investing your life in things that make a difference.

*—Author unknown*

## Achieving With Personal Time Assessment

*Complete the following blanks.*

***What do I wish I had more time for?***

________________________________________

________________________________________

________________________________________

________________________________________

***What would I like to spend less time on?***

______________________________________________

______________________________________________

______________________________________________

______________________________________________

***What would I like to have happening in my life that is not happening now?***

______________________________________________

______________________________________________

______________________________________________

______________________________________________

## Achieving by Analyzing My Typical Work Day

**Here are some important analytical questions.**

*What went right today?*

*What went wrong today?*

*What time did I start my top-priority task?*

*What patterns can I see from my typical day?*

*What habits must I clearly change?*

*What was the least productive period of my day?*

*What was the most productive period of my day?*

*Who caused my interruptions?*

*What caused my interruptions?*

*What activities needed more time today?*

*What activities could I have spent less time on today?*

*What activities could have been delegated? To whom?*

*What could I have started on earlier in my day? How?*

*How can I eliminate my three biggest time wasters?*

## Achieving by Controlling Your Time

Control your time! Don't be controlled by others. Many people are controlled by the events and activities of others. They are always running to the drum beat of another.

Charles J. Givens gives us a strategy for the successful use of time. He says to ask yourself *"Do I"* questions.[10]

*They are as follows:*

"Do I…."

- Plan my daily objectives and activities?
- Prioritize my daily activities?
- Show up on time?
- Start on time?
- Refuse to get drawn into confrontations?
- Eliminate interruptions, even from relatives and friends?
- Separate my emotions from events that occur around me?
- Maintain a positive, "can-do" attitude?
- Plan my work, then "work my plan"?

🕔 Complete my day by prioritizing my activities for the following day?

## Achieving by Activity Planning

- Identify specific activities
- Set priorities for activities
- Estimate the time needed for each activity
- Schedule the activity

## Achieving by Noting Unproductive Activities

✓ ______________________________
✓ ______________________________
✓ ______________________________
✓ ______________________________
✓ ______________________________
✓ ______________________________
✓ ______________________________
✓ ______________________________
✓ ______________________________
✓ ______________________________
✓ ______________________________
✓ ______________________________
✓ ______________________________
✓ ______________________________
✓ ______________________________

## Achieving by Getting Control of Your Time

The most important thing a person can do is to get control of his/her time. Disorganization, feeling overwhelmed, finding too little time to do too many things, being over-extended, etc. are all areas that relate to each other.

If you find yourself in this category, here are some tips to help you get back in control of your time:

***Avoid.*** Avoid all of those terrible time killers. Telephone interruptions, drop-in visitors, and meetings are common time wasters. But indecision, procrastination, and a lack of self-discipline, as well as boredom, frustration, indifference, and resentment, are the most damaging time killers.

***Choose.*** Choose your critical chores and obligations. Set a time frame. List items to be accomplished by lunch, and then those things which should be done in the afternoon. Stick to your list.

***Clean.*** Clean your desk. When was the last time you actually saw the top of your desk? If you have a problem keeping track of things, projects, papers, lists, etc. than you need a cleaner desk, cleaner files and some organization in your life. A poor system (messy desk, cluttered files, etc.) for organization will rob you of efficiency, waste your valuable time and hamper your ability to serve customers well. Use an "in-basket." Make everyone use it. Don't let them dump on your desk, chair, etc. Empty your "in-basket" once each day.

***Delegate.*** Convince yourself that it's not necessary to do everything yourself. You can still be certain that things are being done the way you want them to be when you delegate.

***Paper.*** Get rid of it! Some paperwork can be delegated. Status reports, general inquiries, research, etc., can often be completed by someone else. Let them! Much of your "In" basket should be going "Out" to your associates. For involved projects, delegation is essential. Break up larger segments into smaller segments and let someone else complete the task. Do the final compilation and analysis yourself — but not the initial leg work.

Other paperwork can be dumped immediately. Just because it is addressed to you does not mean you must keep it. Use the trash can or recycling bin liberally. If you can't see any immediate use for the information, get rid of it. If the paperwork that comes across your path cannot be delegated or dumped, then just do it!

File it, route it, place a phone call, whatever seems necessary, but do something and get it out of your life! If you can't complete the project associated with a particular piece of paper, label a file folder, place it in your drawer and make a note to yourself. It is better to have one list than several stacks on your desk, chair, bookcase, and floor, etc.

Controlling the volume of paper is the first step to getting organized. It will help you to do your job better and more efficiently.

***Pass.*** Pass on work that limits the time you need to finish your major responsibilities. Learn to say "no" to requests. You can't say "yes" to everything without spreading yourself too thin. Decide what you must do — and want to do — and say "*no*" to all other requests. Allow yourself to say "no" to the tasks that will cause you to fall further behind in your primary duties. Your friends, customers, associates, and others will understand if you explain that other work is more critical at that moment. Offer support and assistance, but pass on the request unless it is more important than your current task.

***Perform.*** Complete just one item at a time. Don't jump around from one uncompleted task to another. You'll relieve tension as you finish each item. A sense of accomplishment will counteract your sense of being overwhelmed.

***Prevent.*** Prevent burnout and frustration by setting a steady pace. Sometimes a regular pace that allows for some accomplishment is better than a faster one that makes you spin your wheels. Time management is a critical skill for continued success. Everyone has the same amount of time. Don't spend yours treading in circles that turn your days into zeros.

***Procrastinating.*** Don't do it. Get those unpleasant chores done first — if they're important. Divide large tasks into smaller ones. Set reasonable deadlines. Reward yourself when you accomplish something.

***Spread.*** Don't spread yourself too thin by trying to do too many things at once. You must set priorities for each day and, if necessary, each hour. Get the most important things done first.

***Telephone.*** Don't be a slave to the phone. Screen your calls. Use an voice mail when you don't want to be disturbed. Schedule a telephone hour to return all calls.

# Achieving by Planning Your Work

***Get It Done!***

Detailed planning is absolutely necessary. With proper planning you can gather the necessary materials, systems and procedures and utilize spare moments for the preparation of coming events.

Planning for five or six days helps you realize how your work fits into the overall weekly picture. This takes the rush out of life by giving you time to fit your priorities into a manageable weekly schedule. Plan your work. Get it done!

***G – Goals:*** When planning your week, ask these questions. What are the goals and objectives you would like to accomplish this week? What results do you want to see by the end of the week? Write them down and rank them by importance.

***E – Events:*** What events must take place this week in order to achieve your goals? List the necessary events and activities and put them in the order or sequence in which they will occur.

***T – Time:*** How much time will it take for you to complete each activity? To plan realistically, allow yourself more time than you think you will actually need. This builds in a certain amount of flexibility if unexpected problems develop.

Look at your calendar and determine when you can do each activity. Most people underestimate the power of a schedule. But rarely does anything get accomplished without scheduling specific time for that event to occur.

***I - "I" Discipline:*** Get yourself going. Decide that "I will" follow my schedule this week. "I will" stay to complete the events and activities as I have planned. "I will" be persistent. "I will" complete my weekly objectives.

***T – Task:*** Stay on Task! Don't get discouraged. Focus, Focus, Focus!

***D - Divide & Conquer:*** Break big jobs into small parts and complete the entire job by working on one piece at a time.

***O – One:*** Do only one job at a time. Finish it, then tackle the next one on your list.

***N - Never Give Up:*** Keep plugging away each day of the week - even if you get sidetracked. If this happens, get back on task and start with the next event. Some time may be lost, but the sooner you begin again, the more productive the week will be.

***E - Expect the Unexpected:***

Interruptions are common. Increase your time margin. Some say to add at least a 10% fudge factor to every appointment.

## Dealing With Too Little Time

What can you do when you run out of time? Are there some options to consider? Yes there are....consider these.

- ***Working Faster:*** *often produces more problems*
- ***Working Longer:*** *results in physical & mental fatigue*
- ***Getting Organized:*** *some definite value*
- ***Making Choices:*** *for the best results*

### *Wrong Criteria For Allocating Your Time*

**What should your priorities be? Here are some typical problem areas.**

- Arrival order is how we determine our workday.

- Consequences, good or bad, determine what we give our time to.
- Crises and the so-called emergencies of others dictate our day.
- Demands by others get our first response.
- Fun tasks come first.
- Habit determines our day.
- Interesting projects grab our first response.
- Missed or approaching deadlines demand our response.
- Projects which we can complete faster get our attention first.
- Random selection gets us involved in the day.
- Response is on the basis of the one who wants it.
- Small jobs are tackled first.
- Socially expedient activities come before urgent needs.
- Tasks that provide immediate closure get our attention first.
- Things we like come before things we do not like.
- Unplanned tasks come before planned tasks.
- We begin projects we have resources for.
- We want to do the easy jobs before we do the difficult jobs.

## Achieving Through Self Management

Making the most of your day is very important. It requires your day to be very efficient and productive. That is not always so easy. Everyone experiences "time robbers" — defined as inefficient meetings; procrastination; a disorganized desk; interruptions from the telephone or unexpected guests; failure to plan ahead; or numerous other unplanned uses of your time.

These "time eaters" waste your time at the office causing you to fall behind on your work or at least prevent you from being more productive. They can rob you of your personal time also. You can make the best of these unforeseen circumstances and reclaim precious lost hours by managing your time in a realistic and productive manner.

## *Successful people manage their time!*

Each of us has exactly the same 24 hours in the day. Successful people manage their time! They set priorities and then allow their priorities to manage their calendar. Ineffective individuals are often mastered by the loudest voices, the urgent and the unplanned. They are ruled by pressures, not by priorities.

Most people find time management troublesome because they don't understand the basic principle of time. People react to circumstance by being controlled — ideally, they should control circumstance.

Think of time as your personal resource and you will be more likely to use it wisely. It you think of it as a valuable and scarce resource, you will most likely take steps to prevent its wasteful use.

If you "blow" a day, it's gone. You can't save up time. If you waste time, you also waste opportunity. The key to managing your time is developing the philosophy and the habits that put you in control of your life.

A person must know his/her purpose for the week, month and year. The ability to know just what one must accomplish in any given period of time is the very essence of time management.

Having a clear sense of purpose or vision of what you must accomplish is the first step. Knowing this, one can then evaluate every event, every activity and every conversation and determine whether or not it moved you closer to your goal.

Having determined your purpose for a larger period of time, you must have a clear idea of its effect on the present day. What are the things that I need to be involved in today that will fit into my overall purpose.

Once you know how today fits into your larger plan, make simple daily plans.

This can be accomplished through simple lists of attainable daily goals. Take each thing on your list one step at a time. Point all of your conversation, events and personal efforts toward that direction.

Don't try to do everything at once or you'll wind up not completing anything. It is impossible to focus on all that you must do in a given year, month, week or even a day. Some people get little accomplished in a given period of time because they are unable to get focused.

Unorganized people usually fall far short of their potential in life, because they are often unfocused, overextended and constantly facing multiple challenges.

It has been noted that animal trainers carry a stool when they go into the cage of lions. Why is this? The trainers always have their whips and pistols at their side for protection. But according to some, the stool is the trainers' most important tool.

The trainer holds the stool by the seat and thrust the legs toward the animals' face. The animal apparently tries to focus on all four legs at once. In the attempt to focus on all four, a kind of paralysis overwhelms the animal, and it becomes tame, weak and disable because its attention is fragmented.

A simple formula for getting organized is this: Focus on one activity at a time. In order to determine what that activity should be, three questions need to be asked before picking from a wide array of possibilities.

1. First, how important is this task?
2. Second, how urgent is it.
3. Third, will focusing on this task take me closer to my predetermined, balanced, personal-family-job purpose and goals?

At the end of the day, review your progress. Did you get it all done? Did you accomplish a significant amount? If not, what were the events that hindered your progress. Are you closer to your weekly & monthly goals as a result of your efforts today?

Effective time management should not be about scheduling every minute of every day. It's not about lots of diaries and time logs. It is about using your time to accomplish what is most important in your life and in your profession.

Author and lecturer, Steven Covey, had the following observations about what it means to be a successful person. He said that successful people lead "balanced" lives. They read the best literature and keep up with current events. They are active socially, having friends. They are active intellectually. They read, watch, observe and learn.

Within the limits of age and health, they are active physically. They have a lot of fun. They enjoy themselves. They are secure and have no need to brag, drop names or borrow strength from past titles or achievements. They are open in communication, simple, direct, non manipulative. They tend to understate rather than to exaggerated.

They are not extremists. They do not make things all or nothing, good or bad and either/or. They think in terms of continuums and priorities. Their actions and attitudes are temperate and wise. They are not workaholics, fanatics, crash dieters, pleasure addicts or martyrs. They're not slavishly chained to their plans and schedules. They live in the present, carefully plan the future and adapt to unexpected changes. They are willing to admit and then forget mistakes.

Some people become slaves to time. *Balance is the key.* Some weeks in my life, it seems every minute of every day and night are totally taken up with things that do not necessarily bring me closer to my purpose and goals, either professionally or personally.

I find myself doing some things just because others expect it of me. Just how many social activities can one attend? How many errands must be run that others could do for themselves. How many meetings require your attendance that could be avoided, or even done away with altogether. Are you caught up in time gridlock? *If so, here are a few tips:*

Decide what you want out of life. Assess all of your activities. If they add significantly to your life keep them. If not, dump them.

Understand your limits both physically and mentally. Don't take on more than you can handle. It's not necessary and not life changing. If you burn out sooner, you'll be of no help to anyone later.

Build cushions of time into your schedule. If you don't, you'll end the day/week/month/year out of breath, out of energy, out of focus and maybe even totally burned out. Reduce the daily tension, and increase your effectiveness by prioritizing what is really necessary in today's schedule.

Find a slower pace. Some people are addicted to rushing; rushing here, rushing there, etc. Know the difference between necessary haste and pure impatience. Before you commit to a new activity or involvement, subtract an old one.

## Achieving Personal Success With Efficient Use of Time

### *A Special Day*

Declare a personal "Get It Done" day. This might help you to finish the little unpleasant or boring tasks that you have been carrying around on your "to do" list for some time. Let's face it — we all procrastinate. On a daily basis we put off whatever we don't want to tackle, doing only the tasks that we like and absolutely must take care of. But then all of those odds and ends pile up until we begin to feel pressured to get them done.

Having a monthly "Get It Done" day could be the time to finish just one bigger task or several smaller projects. You might clean the garage, clean out your office desk, update computer files, or reorganize and update your contact or address list. Make note of this special day in your daily planner — you'll find it easier to get it done.

All kinds of sophisticated tools are available for purchase, but if you don't use them or rely upon them, they all are worthless. The simplest tool is a piece of scratch paper and a pencil. But if you don't turn that into a "to do" list and use it daily, even it will not help you get organized. Successful time management today means finding a system that works for you. Each person is different, and no one system will work well for everyone.

***Analyze Your Time***

Time is a tremendous resource available to all of us. Since it is perishable and irreplaceable, it is important to analyze how we spend it. Is it spent in productive ways, or is there a lot of ill-spent time within our schedule? Occasionally spend some time tracking your activities. How much time is spent in travel that could be avoided? Could you make four stops in one trip instead of making four trips with one stop each?

***Become a Dictator***

How many things have you forgotten to do because you didn't jot them down when they came to mind? Purchase an inexpensive "Voice It" recorder. Save time by recording all letters, memos, or ideas that pop into you mind. Your dictation skills will increase with practice.

***Control the Phone***

The telephone is a tool. Don't let it become a thief of your time. First of all, don't mix working hours with personal business. Keep yourself on task during your work day and keep focused on the business of the day.

Secondly, don't let others waste your time whether it be personal friends or other unsolicited calls to your office. On any given day, at least ten or twelve calls come in for me which are screened out by our receptionist.

Additionally, some calls get through after telling the call screener that I am expecting their call or they are returning my call. When the caller begins his/her "canned solicitation," I immediately hang up. There is no need to be polite since he/she got through to me by not telling the truth to the receptionist or in some other devious way.

If a call comes through when you are unavailable and is not urgent, schedule a part of your day for returning calls. This will enable you to concentrate on more pressing matters at hand without having to start and stop the same project multiple times during your day.

One day when I was away at a much needed seminar, I returned to my office at the end of the day to find 48 different paper messages on my desk from people trying to speak with me. This was in addition to the voice mail, cell phone and 150+ email messages that I received on that day. Control the telephone, screen your calls, and focus on the core business of your position. If you do so, you'll get a lot more done!

***Delegate***

Successful leaders don't try to do everything themselves. However, they do make sure that it does get done. You may not be the best person to get the job done. Sometimes others can get it done quicker, better, and more accurately than you could have.

Don't be afraid to delegate. Convince yourself that it's not necessary to do everything yourself. You can still be certain that things are being done the way you want them to be when you delegate.

Create a communication record for each subordinate. Record each item you delegate and the deadline that was agreed to. List each item you plan to discuss the next time you sit down together. Follow-up and keep your staff accountable.

***Develop a Regular Work Schedule***

Many people hate to be tied to a regular schedule. Some may even feel that it cuts down on their spontaneity and creativity. With the help of a schedule, however, you will find that you have less resistance to difficult jobs and are mentally prepared for each task. Set appointments, schedule phone calls and allow time to complete projects.

The most important thing is to have a clear idea of your priorities and to spend as much time as possible on your high-priority items. Record your goals in a daily planner that contains a prioritized list of objectives. Update the list and check off items as they are finished.

### *Do a Clean Sweep*

Periodically, clean up areas that are no longer necessary. These include computer files, paper files, marketing brochures, catalogs, etc. There are any number of reasons for discarding an item. If that piece of paper does not require any action on your part, toss it. It probably exists elsewhere.

### *Do Related Jobs Together.*

Each time you change to a different type of work, your mind must change gears. Sometimes as much as 20 minutes can be required to make that transition. When you do work that has related aspects together, you cut down on transition lag.

The more related characteristics that tasks have in common, the greater the benefit of grouping these types of work together. Group your telephone calls to avoid having an entire day punctuated by endless telephone interruptions.

### *Do the Right Things*

Peter Drucker says, "Of late I've been doing less but achieving more." Form habits which do the right things. Habits are first formed by the activities in which we participate. After formation, habits then form us and our present and future.

Not to consciously form good habits, is to unconsciously form bad ones. No habit is an automatic action nor is it an instinct. Habits do not just happen, they are caused. Habits are acquired reactions to previous choices. If you can determine the original cause of a habit, it is probably within your power to change it.

Do you want to be successful in the management of your time? Forming habits that benefit your personal and business goals will help you achieve success. People who fail often times have formed habits that "do the wrong things." Sometimes success or failure in life begins with early habit-forming choices. The harvest that we reap in our lives can often be measured by the attitudes and habits which we cultivate.

***Don't get caught in needless conversation***

If you find yourself caught up in needless conversation, get out of it quick! Simply state the obvious — you have to get back to work. Peers often need someone to take the lead and break it off . . . or even better, not allow it to get started.

***Don't Procrastinate***

Get right on all of those unpleasant chores. If they are a priority, do them first. Divide the larger tasks into smaller ones. Reward yourself when you get a few of the tasks accomplished…take a quick walk, grab a cup of coffee or tea, have a snack, etc.

Mark Twain is credited with saying this, "The secret of getting ahead is getting started. The secret of getting started is breaking your complex overwhelming tasks into small manageable tasks, and then starting on the first one." I concur!

***Establish Weekly Objectives***

Know what you are trying to accomplish with your life and determine how this week will help you accomplish those goals. Leave your week, month or year to chance and chances are you won't like the way your life is lived. Write a general priority list of all projects and deadlines and assess the importance of each. This will guide you to get priorities completed first.

### *Extended Time*

You can add thirty minutes to each day by rising just ten minutes earlier, lunching just ten minutes less, and retiring just ten minutes later. This will give you an extra 183 hours per year.

If dedicated to a specific project or goal, (reading to your children, writing a book, enjoying a hobby, prayer and meditation, etc.) think of what you could accomplish each year.

Goals that are out of sight are out of mind. Encourage yourself and others to be prepared to present an abbreviated version of their goals on a moment's notice. Each day, ask yourself: What have I done today to bring me closer to achieving my goals? This discipline keeps the pressure on you to be more goal oriented.

How much time do you spend sitting in lobbies, waiting for appointments, or listening to unscheduled guests? If these things cannot be avoided, involve yourself in productive paperwork or reading instead of just waiting while the time passes.

Measure your time for a few days, weeks, etc. Analyze how you spend your time. Note problem areas and create a time management procedure that increases your productive time. Be committed to improving your time management skills.

If it is outdated, get rid of it. If it is just "miscellaneous" information for possible consideration later, dump it. Believe me, if it is important enough, it will show up again. Cleaning up the physical clutter in your life will also serve to clean up the items cluttering your thought processes. Keep the clutter out of your life!

### *Keep a Clean Desk*

Get rid of any paperwork that you do not use on a daily basis. Store it, drawer it, or toss it. Too often, incoming and outgoing mail gets thrown into one pile. The result? Complete chaos. Designate a specific desk space or bin to keep incoming mail until you have time to deal with it.

For outgoing mail, set up another bin where it is easily visible as you leave your office or work area. Work from a clean desk. Clutter is not only distracting, it makes it too easy to lose things.

***Learn to rest creatively***

The mind and body soon tire of working at one type of job or in one place or position. Fatigue begins to set in. Frequently all that is needed is a momentary change of pace. Sometimes you can take five minutes to think through a program or read an article and then return to the task at hand.

***Learn to Say "No"***

If something doesn't fit with your goals, objectives, plans, priorities or service to others, learn to say "NO." You cannot say "yes" to everything without spreading yourself too thin. If you give yourself to many things at once, none of the tasks will be done with accuracy and completeness.

You must set priorities for each day and, if necessary, each hour. Get the most important things done first. Decide upon what you must do in order to fulfill your business and personal responsibilities and "just say no" to all other requests.

***Management Tools***

Despite the availability of many great organizational tools, many people still don't complete their projects on time. Even a simple "to do" list won't work unless you take the time each day to keep it current. Organize with time management tools only if you will continuously use them.

Or simply organize the papers in stackable bins labeled TO FILE, TO COPY and TO ROUTE. Then, of course, there is the wastebasket — don't be afraid to make use of it. Continuously refine what goes on top of your desk. Don't use the desk as a perpetual filing cabinet.

Clean up your desk each evening before leaving the office. You'll find it much easier to get a productive start the next day. Nothing can seem as overwhelming as clutter when you arrive to work in the morning.

***Organizational Strategies***

When choosing organizational methods, there is no right or wrong approach. It really doesn't make much difference how you do it; the most important thing is to do it continuously and in a consistent matter. The purpose of an organizational strategy is to order your personal time and life. If you constantly feel "cluttered," out of time, and out of control, some sort of organized effort must be subscribed to in order to put you back on top of matters.

Organization by itself has no value. But when it helps to put you in control of your life so that you can be an effective and productive person, it becomes very valuable to you personally and to those whom you serve.

***Over-Commitment***

The great coach of the Green Bay Packers, Vince Lombardi, once inspired his football team in this manner. While discussing the impact of exhaustion on human courage, he noted that, "Fatigue makes cowards of us all." What a profound and exacting message he had.

How often have you been overworked, over-tired, and found yourself beginning to whine, gripe, blame others, or verbally hurt those you love, simply because you have tried so hard to please others by giving your time and resources? When a person is "over-committed" he or she is no fun to be around.

When over-fatigued, and feeling the pressure to produce in those moments when you should be resting or even sleeping, a time of reflection may be in order. The time has come to stop kidding yourself; this hectic pace is not simply a temporary problem – it's probably a habitual lifestyle that you have learned.

Time usually proves that the rush is never over. One thing leads to another and the temporary pressures gradually develop into a long-term lifestyle. Don't let it continue to happen! Learn the secret of living one day at a time. Everything does not have to be done today.

Workaholics, like myself, push themselves to get everything done today. Guard against over-commitment. Don't let others program your life so that you consume your last ounce of energy and use up all the free moments in the day. Learn to say no gracefully but firmly. If you happen to be a workaholic, develop the capacity to do nothing. sometimes the body has more sense than the mind. Pay attention to it. Learn to say no. be stingy with your time.

***Paper Handling***

In an ideal world, the only papers on your desk would be those you are working on. But most of the documents on our desks need to be filed, copied, tossed or routed elsewhere. Handle each paper only once if at all possible. Separate your papers into folders, based upon the importance to you.

***Post Your Goals***

Put both your long-range and short-range goals in writing. It's difficult to hit a target you cannot see. The goal-setting process alone is practically a guarantee that you will achieve greater results. Post your goals.

***Prioritize Lists***

When prioritizing your day/week/month/year, ask yourself this question. "What do I want to accomplish by the end of the period?" After a period of time has come and gone, what do you want to see? I like to prioritize my list in this fashion. I label it "NIP." When it comes to those things which would demand my time and attention, I "NIP" it.

1. Necessary:task must be done
2. Important:task should be done
3. Possible: task worthwhile

Each night , write down three or four tasks from your necessary folder. Keep the list handy. Try to complete as many of these as possible the very next day.

***Review Your Agenda***

Leave enough time at the end of your day to review what you've planned for the next one. Think about what you'll need tomorrow. Prepare yourself physically and mentally. At the end of the week, verify scheduled appointments and prepare your strategy for next week.

***Saving Time***

Instead of inviting people to your office, visit them. That way you can leave when you're ready to end the meeting. Arrange your office so you don't face the door. If you don't make eye contact with people who pass by, you can avoid some unnecessary conversation.

Stand up when a visitor enters your office — and stay standing. If you don't invite people to sit down, the business will get finished sooner. When someone interrupts your work, let the person know you're willing to talk — but not indefinitely. Tell the interrupter that you must be back at work on your project by a specific time. When conversations turn to social topics, bring them to a close. This doesn't mean you should be anti-social — just save the socializing for lunch and breaks.

***Schedule Personal Quiet Time***

Schedule quiet time. Deep thinking can only occur during quiet time. Inform everyone around you about the period of time in which you are not to be interrupted. Block out time to dream, plan, review goals, review purpose, etc. Schedule it in your weekly calendar just as you would any other important appointment.

***The "To Do" List***

Rewrite your "to do" list daily — always keep it current. Revise it at the end of the evening before you retire for the day. List the jobs that need to be done that very next day. Number them in the order of their importance. Then, visualize the materials that these jobs will require.

Subconsciously, you will begin to prepare for the many tasks that will require your attention the following day. Prioritize your "to do" list. Before you begin each day, review the "to do" list to determine which items can be delegated. Of the items not delegated, discipline yourself to do the most critical activities, first by numbering each item from most to least critical. Be sure to get numbers 1-10 behind you before moving on to 11-20. A daily "to do" list is a must. A weekly "to do" list is advised. A monthly "to do" list will help you stay on track.

***Use the Circular File***

Use your wastebasket! Don't bother to open mail that you didn't solicit or mail unrelated to your business needs. I save at least ten to fifteen minutes a day by not opening mail that doesn't affect the way I do business.

Hundreds of pieces of mail — which will not prosper or help the operation of this business — come to my office each week. To sort through it and open it just because it arrives at your desk, is to waste literally days out of every year. Watch your fax mail and e-mail also. Don't feel obligated to open it just because it shows up!

***Value Today***

We tend to categorize time in three areas: Past, Present, Future. While we can learn from history, we cannot change it. It is gone forever. It no longer exists. While we can prepare for the future, it is yet to occur. We cannot use future time. This leaves only the present moment available for our use. Only today... this hour, this minute is available to us.

Only the present moment truly exists. Now is the moment to make the best use of our time. To think that "tomorrow" will be better than "right now" is wishful thinking. Do what you can do to properly use the time available to you now. Now is the appointed time, use it wisely.

Even if the day starts out wrong, don't give up on it. Rethink, retool, regroup, and turn it into a productive event. Forget about discouragement caused through lost time or unexpected events. Make the best of what is left in the day. Nothing is worth more than this day. Today's actions will determine tomorrow's achievements.

***Work Hard in Prime Time***

Every person has a prime time, slowing down time, and lag time. Prime time — Biggest energy burst, premium benefit, push the work out! Lag time — You're slowing down, take some time to relax. Work at a pace that is comfortable for you, but work consistently all day long --you'll get more done.

***Work smarter, not harder***

When inventing the light bulb, Thomas Edison made some 8,000 attempts. Most of us, like Edison, will have periods in our life when we won't be able to function in the most efficient way. But the most important step is to get started. If you don't get started, you can't get it done.

## Achieving Personal Success by Resisting Procrastination

What does it mean to procrastinate? Procrastination means doing low-priority activities rather than high-priority ones. An old proverb says, when all is said and done, more is usually said than done. To procrastinate means to put off doing a task — for no good reason. Impel yourself to get it done. Be tough on self-discipline.

Most procrastination is the result of irrational thinking. You talk yourself into putting off a task, not because it is simply unpleasant, but because it is awful, horrible, UNBEARABLE! Convince yourself instead that the task is worth doing, even if it's hard getting started.

Challenge your excuses for putting the assignment off. For example, if you generally excuse yourself by saying, "But I work so well under pressure," argue that "working under pressure really leaves me harried and tired, and I don't have the time I need to be creative." This type of inner debate can keep you from stalling and works for any excuse, not matter how "logical."

Don't let procrastination be a pleasant experience. If you usually procrastinate by socializing, don't socialize. If you must procrastinate, do it in unpleasant conditions. Lock yourself in your office. No coffee. No visitors. When the fun goes away, the procrastination just might disappear.

Confirmed procrastinators usually work in a feast or famine pattern. One way to fight the tendency is to schedule frequent tasks for regular times. Return telephone calls between 11 and 12 every morning. Answer letters and memos between 9:00 and 9:30.

Procrastination is an emotional problem. Let's take a close look at your habits.

*What things do I tend to put off the most?*

*What things am I currently delaying?*

*Do I know when I am procrastinating?*

*What negative things happen when I choose to delay?*

*What positive things happen when I choose to delay?*

*How do I feel about my procrastination?*

*What causes my procrastination?*

*What can I do to overcome my problem?*

## Are You a Procrastinator?

*Here are some questions to ask yourself.*

*Do I . . .?*

- Put off doing something I have to get done?
- Wait to move until someone forces or strongly encourages me to do something?
- Look for reasons (or excuses) not to do something I should do?
- Fail to complete projects I've started?
- Allow myself pleasant indulgences (oversleeping, overeating, skipping responsibilities)?
- Find that I've run out of time to complete a project properly because I didn't start soon enough?
- Allow obstacles and difficulties to prevent me from completing a project?

If you answered "*yes*" to some of these questions, you should develop some time management strategies. Consider these thoughts to get you going.

Ask yourself, "What is the best use of my time at this moment?" Then, just do it!

*When you kill time, just remember it has no resurrection.*

*Unsuccessful people are ruled by pressure. Successful people are ruled by priorities.*

*The easiest way to start a project is to "start a project."*

# The Principle of Never Giving Up!

## Insight Seven

# The Principle of Never Giving Up!

A lot of people struggle in their quest to build something of themselves. Even the best laid plans can go astray and get off course. In your business life, it will happen for sure. But instead of being overcome by failure, overcome failure by facing it head on and beginning again.

There are any number of biblical characters who ran adrift and became discouraged and wanted to give up. David did, Elijah wanted to, Peter and the disciples wanted to give up, Timothy went through difficult times, as did Paul, Saul and Jonathan and many others.

Let's take a look at a one of these biblical citizens.

**Peter experiences failure but persists.**

**Matthew 26:33-35**

> *Peter replied, "Even if all fall away on account of you, I never will." "I tell you the truth," Jesus answered, "this very night, before the rooster crows, you will disown me three times." But Peter declared, "Even if I have to die with you, I will never disown you." And all the other disciples said the same.*

- Jesus prophecies that all his disciples will fall away from him
- Peter swears that he never will
- Peter says that he will die before disowning Jesus
- all the other disciples say the same thing
- Jesus insists that it will happen before morning
- Jesus says Peter will betray him not one time, but three
- Jesus goes to Gethsemane to pray
- He instructs His disciples to pray
- He returns from prayer to find all of the disciples asleep (Matthew 26:40)
- Judas arrives with a large crowd of armed men
- Jesus is betrayed by Judas with a kiss (Matthew 26:47)
- Jesus is arrested
- Peter follows the crowd at a distance
- the high priest accuses Jesus
- the crowd spots Peter sitting in the courtyard
- they accuse him of being a follower of Christ
- Peter betrays Jesus three times (Matthew 26:70)
- a three-time failure he goes outside and weeps bitterly (Matthew 26:75)
- marvels at the linens in the grave (Luke 24:12)
- saw the risen Christ (Luke 24:39)
- saw Jesus and jumped into the water (John 21:7)
- told by Jesus to feed the sheep (John 21:15-18)
- becomes the recognized leader of the apostles (Acts 1:15-22)
- Peter preaches on the Day of Pentecost (Acts 2:14-41)
- is used by God to perform first miracle (Acts 3:1-4)

**Lessons in persistence from Peter**

- everybody experiences discouragement
- watch what you say in times of discouragement
- everyone is affected by their emotions
- testing is common to all
- circumstances are temporary
- when hope seems gone, we want to give up
- it is important to experience hope
- we need to encourage each other and ourselves
- we must not live by how we feel
- testing is designed to make us stronger
- failure is no respecter of persons
- we can overcome any obstacle
- we can persist and get stronger
- we can always get up again
- we can start over again
- we can win even after failure
- always keep your faith positive
- there is always hope in your future
- failure is not final

# Never Give Up!

**Perseverance & Persistence**

A potentially successful person is often stopped by short term obstacles that either come by personal failures or simply by the twists and turns of life itself. Whether or not these occurrences are short lived or permanent are determined solely by your attitude and approach to them.

Only *you* have the power to say how they will effect your future. What obstacle will stop you from receiving the very best of God's supernatural provision over your life? What roadblock will you encounter that will make you want to give up?

When that happens, do you just give up and say that you have no control over circumstances? Or do you start again with a new attitude that you will continue to strive for excellence?

Persistence, or not quitting after the first personal, spiritual, moral, business or financial failure, is one of the qualities that define people of purpose.

**Ephesians 6:18**

> *With all prayer and petition pray at all times in the Spirit, and with this in view, be on the alert with all perseverance and petition for all the saints.* (NAS)

**Hebrews 12:1**

> *"... us run with perseverance the race marked out for us."*

**2 Peter 1:5-6**

> *For this very reason, make every effort to add to your faith goodness; and to goodness, knowledge; and to knowledge, self-control; and to self-control, perseverance; and to perseverance, godliness.*

**James 1:4**

> *Perseverance must finish its work so that you may be mature and complete, not lacking anything.*

**Revelation 2:19**

*I know your deeds, your love and faith, your service and perseverance, and that you are now doing more than you did at first.*

Sometimes problems seem "impossible". Your tendency may be to think, it can't be done. I should just give up now because I can't do it. But much of our incorrect thinking can be out of panic, a bad attitude or discouragement. We need to align our attitude and thinking with "possibility thinking."

Instead of reflecting on the "impossible," take the "IM" out of impossible and replace it with "I M" (I am) responsible and "I M" (I am) possible. Often times the possible is being blocked in your mind by the "I m" in impossible. Think "I'm Possible" instead of "impossible". Yes, you can do it! Yes, you can overcome any obstacle! Say it out loud now, *"I'm free to pursue my possibilities!"*

You have probably heard how Abraham Lincoln lost every election but one prior to his being elected president of the United States. You may have also read how Thomas Edison failed more than 10,000 times prior to inventing the incandescent light.

However, Edison's view of failure can shed interesting light on the word persistence. Rather than failing, he believed that he succeeded in finding 10,000 ways not to invent the incandescent light. In other words, the process of elimination is a vital part of the invention process.

Edison went on to say that he knew he would soon succeed because he ran out of ways that didn't work. Where would we be today if it were not for Edison's great persistence?

More recent history also points to great examples of persistence. Colonel Sanders was rejected more than a thousand times before his first successful sale of the Kentucky Fried Chicken formula.

Lee Iacocca was fired from the presidency of Ford Motor Company, but his persistence led him on to even greater heights as the chairman of Chrysler Corporation. Thomas Watson, the founder of IBM, when asked about how others could emulate his great success formula, replied simply to increase their rate of failure.

## *Don't Give Up on Yourself*

In other words, trying and failing is a risk one must bear in order to be able to try and succeed. Why? Because personal failure and personal rejection are necessary precursors to your success.

You can beat up on yourself and whine about how you messed up again. You can place the blame on others. Or you can reread Scripture on God's desire to bless you if you will align yourself to the principles of God's Word and make Him your business partner.

You may be thinking how many times you have tried to be successful in the past and failed in one area or another. But it's amazing how many weaknesses and challenges you can overcome if you are persistent.

Persistence is not inherited. It's a state of mind — an attitude. And since it is an attitude, it's something each of us can develop. The first step is knowing exactly what you want. If you have only a vague idea of where you're going, it's easy to give up at the first sign of a business problem. You must have a clear personal goal, an intensive desire to reach it, and a definite plan that shows the past that must be followed.

You can win! *You can be successful! You can achieve personal success!* You can have a successful life! Having faith in God your partner is important, but you must also have faith in yourself. If you believe you can succeed in the areas of improvement you have set for yourself, setbacks along the way won't cause you to give up. You'll seldom reach a goal without stumbling along the way; faith in yourself enables you to get up and keep going even after slipping a bit.

# Perseverance & Persistence

Here is a general guideline for you to apply to your life.

- Plan Purposefully
- Prepare Prayerfully
- Proceed Positively
- Pursue Persistently

### *Perseverance*

Continuance
Decide
Determination
Doggedness
Endurance
Fix on
Fortitude
Immovability
Make up your mind
Perseverance
Persistence
Purpose
Resolve
Settle on
Stamina
Steadfastness
Tenacity
Unchanging
Unwavering

**Antonyms**

backward
doubt
fluctuation
hesitation
indecision
misgiving
oscillate
palpitate
puzzling
questioning
uncertainty
vacillate
vacillation
varying
wavering

The power to hold on when faced with difficulty or failure, the power to endure - this is the song of the overcomer. Persistence is the ability to face defeat again and again without giving up – to push on in the face of personal shortcomings and failure, knowing that victory can be yours. Persistence means taking pains to overcome every obstacle, and to do what's necessary to begin again and again.

"Failure may look like a fact, but it's only an opinion. Successful people believe that mistakes are just feedback. It's not how far you fall but how high you bounce that makes all the difference."[11]

Success in anything in life requires dogged perseverance. Before you can expect the supernatural provision from God, you must be careful that your entire life is based upon biblical principles. Whether in the business world or your personal world, patience, persistence and perseverance is a condition for improvement and ultimate blessing or success.

When you fail, when you stumble, get up, get going and get started again and again. It is what athletes do, it is what business men and women do, it is what husbands and wives do, and it should be what all Christians do. Let's look at some examples of what others have done when it comes to achieving success through personal self-discipline and persistence.

Some of the greatest and most successful people were persistent until life gave them a break. They continued to press on and eventually won because they refused to give up in self defeat and pity.

**Malcolm Forbes**, the late editor-in-chief of Forbes magazine, one of the most successful business publications in the world, failed to make the staff of the school newspaper when he was an undergraduate at Princeton University.

After years of progressive hearing loss, by age 46 German composer **Ludwig van Beethoven** had become completely deaf. Nevertheless, he wrote his greatest music, including five symphonies, during his later years.

After **Fred Astaire's** first screen test, a 1933 memo from the MGM testing director said: "Can't act. Slightly bald. Can dance a little." Astaire kept that memo over the fireplace in his Beverly Hills home.

An expert said of famous football coach **Vince Lombardi**: "He possesses minimal football knowledge. Lacks motivation."

**Louisa May Alcott**, the author of "Little Women," was advised by her family to find work as a servant or seamstress.

**Beethoven** handled the violin awkwardly and preferred playing his own compositions instead of improving his technique. His teacher called him hopeless as a composer.

The teacher of famous opera singer **Enrico Caruso** said Caruso had no voice at all and could not sing.

**Walt Disney** was fired by a newspaper for lacking ideas. He also went bankrupt several times before he built Disneyland.

Eighteen publishers turned down **Richard Bach's** 10,000-word story about a soaring seagull before Macmillan finally published it in 1970. By 1975, "Jonathan Livingston Seagull" had sold more than seven million copies in the U.S. alone.

Dennis Waitley graphically states, "Most people are like an oak tree in a flower pot; they never grow to their full potential." He states that people tend to remain cramped by poor self-belief and compressed by negative self-talk. They list reasons why they can't do it. Few launch into the exhilarating experience of breaking their own expectations with a "Yes I can" attitude.

Leonard Ravenhill tells a fascinating story about a group of tourists in a European village. One of them asked an elderly villager, "Have any great people been born in this village?" The old villager paused and then replied, "No! Only babies."

Successful people stretch for success . . . they dig deep into the possibilities of their God-given potential.

Successful people are not better than other people; they are ordinary people who have extraordinary attitudes . . . they are the people who carry the "Yes I Can" attitude into everything they do. Remember Sir Winston Churchill who said, "If you believe you can, you will. If you believe you can't, you won't. Either way it's your choice."

## You are never too old!

Everyone has heard of the man named Colonel Sanders. But few know how he became such a resounding success. At the age of 65 years, he found himself broke and alone. He received his first Social Security check for $97.00 and used it to begin promoting a chicken recipe everyone seemed to enjoy.

He started knocking on doors, telling restaurant owners his story: "I've got a great chicken recipe and I think if you use it, it'll increase your sales." Many closed the door on his face and his idea. They were too busy making the next meal to listen to a positive thinking 65-year-old salesman. But Colonel Sanders persisted — he believed he could and would do it. He focused on how to tell his story more effectively, how to get better results.

Finally, his ***"Yes I Can"*** attitude paid off. After one thousand and nine refusals he heard his first "yes." He had spent two years driving across America in an old, beat-up car, sleeping in the back seat in his rumpled white suit, getting up each day, tired and discouraged.

But he continued to believe in his product and that someday somebody would listen. Two years of "no's"! One thousand and nine "no's"! That's why there is a KFC today.

In 1954 Ray Kroc was 52 years old and making his living selling milkshake machines in southern California when he discovered his future. Kroc liked what he saw when he visited the hamburger stands of his good customers, the McDonald brothers. First, he bought the franchise rights from them; then seven years later, when he was 59, he bought the whole company for $14 million.

When he died in 1984, his personal stake in McDonald's was worth about $500 million. And he began the whole adventure at just about the age when some people are beginning to think about retirement. Ray A. Kroc, of McDonald's Corporation, posted this quote from President Coolidge on his wall:

> *"Nothing in the world can take the place of persistence. Talent will not; nothing is more common than unsuccessful men with talent. Genius will not; unrewarded genius is almost a proverb. Education will not; the world is full of educated derelicts. Persistence and determination alone are omnipotent."*

Success is connected with action. Successful people keep moving. They make mistakes, but they don't quit. Real courage is when you know you're licked before you begin, but you begin anyway and see it through no matter what.

Age isn't always a factor in your success or failure. Consider some more famous examples.

- Actor George Burns won his first Oscar at 80.

- Golda Meir was 71 when she became Prime Minister of Israel.
- At age 96, playwright George Bernard Shaw broke his leg when he fell out of a tree he was trimming in his backyard.
- Painter Grandma Moses didn't start painting until she was 80 years old. She completed over 1,500 paintings after that; 25% of those were produced when she was past 100.
- Michelangelo was 71 when he painted the Sistine Chapel.
- Physician and humanitarian Albert Schweitzer was still performing operations in his African hospital at 89.
- Charles Carlson, developed the process of photocopying in 1938 but had to persevere for 21 years before the first Xerox copier finally was manufactured.
- Chuck Yeager, on his first flight as a passenger, threw up all over the back seat. He vowed never to go back up again — yet later became the first man to break the sound barrier.
- A woman once said to the great violinist Fritz Kreisler after a recital, "I'd give my life to play as beautifully as you!" "Madam," Kreisler replied, "I have."

Experiencing success is always connected with action. Successful people keep moving. They make mistakes, but they don't quit! Winners stretch for success . . . they dig deep into the possibilities of their God-given potential!

When you feel that being persistent is a difficult task, think of the bee. A red clover blossom contains less than one eighth of a grain of sugar; 7,000 grains are required to make one pound of honey. A bee, flitting here and there must visit 56,000 clover heads for one pound of honey; and there are about sixty flower tubes to each clover head. When a bee performs that operation 60 times (x) 56,000 or 3,360,000 times, it secures enough sweetness for only one pound of honey.

## "And Then Some!"

A prominent athlete summed up his fabulous success in three simple words . . . "and then some!" "I discovered at an early age," he said, that most of the differences between average and top athletes could be explained in three words. The top athletes did what was expected . . . and then some! The top athletes exercised hard work . . . and then some! They were disciplined . . . and then some! They gave their very best . . . and then some! They always met expectations . . . and then some! They reached to the heights of their human potential — and then some. It was the "*and then some*" that turned mediocrity into excellence.

It's a rare person who doesn't get discouraged. Whether it happens to us or to a friend we're trying to cheer up, the answer centers around one word: perseverance. The value of ***courage***, ***persistence***, and ***perseverance*** has rarely been illustrated more convincingly than in the life story of this man.

| | |
|---|---|
| Failed in business | (age 22) |
| Ran for legislature–defeated | (age 23) |
| Again failed in business | (age 24) |
| Elected to legislature | (age 25) |
| Sweetheart died | (age 26) |
| Had a nervous breakdown | (age 27) |
| Defeated for Speaker | (age 29) |
| Defeated for Elector | (age 31) |
| Defeated for Congress | (age 34) |
| Elected to Congress | (age 37) |
| Defeated for Congress | (age 39) |
| Defeated for Senate | (age 46) |
| Defeated for Vice President | (age 47) |
| Defeated for Senate | (age 49) |
| Elected President | (age 51) |

**That's the record of Abraham Lincoln.**

# Quotes About Success

**Here are some inspirational "success" quotes.**

*I do not think there is any other quality so essential to success of any kind as the quality of perseverance. It overcomes almost everything, even nature.*

*—John D. Rockefeller*

*What this power is I cannot say; all I know is that it exists and it becomes available only when a man is in that state of mind in which he knows exactly what he wants and is fully determined not t to quit until he finds it.*

*—Alexander Graham Bell*

*Our greatest glory is not in never falling, but in rising every time we fall.*

*—Confucius*

*History has demonstrated that the most notable winners usually encountered heartbreaking obstacles before they triumphed. They won because they refused to become discouraged by their defeats.*

*—B.C. Forbes*

*Success…seems to be connected with action. Successful men keep moving. They make mistakes, but they don't quit.*

*—Conrad Hilton*

*Success seems to be largely a matter of hanging on after others have let go.*

*—William Feather*

*Effort only fully releases its reward after a person refuses to quit.*

*—Napoleon Hill*

*Most people give up just when they're about to achieve success. They quit on the one yard line. They give up at the last minute of the game one foot from a winning touch down.*

*—H. Ross Perot*

*It's the constant and determined effort that breaks down all resistance, sweeps away all obstacles.*

*—Claude M. Bristol*

*The majority of men meet with failure because of their lack of persistence in creating new plains to take the place of those which fail.*

*—Napoleon Hill*

*Few things are impossible to diligence and skill... Great works are performed not by strength, but perseverance.*

*—Samuel Johnson*

*Success is failure turned inside out, the silver tint of the clouds of doubt, and you never can tell how close you are, it may be near when it seems so far. So stick to the fight when you're hardest hit, it's when things seem worse, that you must not quit.*

*—Unknown*

*He conquers who endures.*

*—Persius*

*The rewards for those who persevere far exceed the pain that must precede the victory.*

*—Ted Engstrom and R. Alec Mackenzie*

*If you can force your heart and nerve and sinew to serve your turn long after they are gone, and so hold on when there is nothing in you Except the will which says to them: "Hold on!"*

*—Rudyard Kipling*

# The Principle of Giving Back

## Insight Eight

# The Principle of Giving Back

*If a man is naturally selfish or arrogant or greedy, the money brings that out, that is all."*
—Henry Ford

Is having a lot of money the key to everything? Does money bring happiness? Does money bring solutions to life's problems? If you had a limitless amount of money and could buy anything you wanted, what would you buy? When would you stop buying, gathering, grasping and grabbing? Our wealth does not come from what we grab in life, but from what we give in life. Don't be a grabber (a taker), be a giver. Be generous!

Some of the wealthiest men in the world gathered in 1923 at the Edgewater Beach Hotel in Chicago. This group of seven was worth more than the entire US Treasury in their time. These were great financial men with records of success who had achieved great prosperity.

But this was not the end of their story. Within twenty-five years the president of the largest steel company had died penniless. A millionaire wheat speculator had also become poor. Another, who was the president of the New York Stock Exchange, had already spent many years in prison. Yet another of the wealthy seven who was a member of the president's cabinet had spent time in prison, but was pardoned so that he could die at home. The fifth of the seven committed suicide and the sixth man, who headed one of the world's largest companies also had taken his life. And the seventh, and last of the world's richest men, took his life.

Will your money become your blessing or your curse? Can money buy happiness? Can it buy contentment? How about peace of mind? Contrast the previous men of wealth with the founder of the Quaker Oats Company who gave 70 percent of his income to God.

Or contrast the Chicago Seven to the wealthy father of many nations. Abraham was a great man of faith, but also a very wealthy individual. Solomon was probably the richest man of his day. Barnabas, an early New Testament local church leader, was also very wealthy but used his money and affluence to extend the Kingdom of God.

James 5:1-3 speaks to the wealthy who would use their money for personal gratification. He tells them that they will weep and howl because of all the misery that is coming upon them. He boldly says that their gold and silver is plagued, and their precious metals will soon rust. James points out how foolish it is to value and esteem one's riches so highly and in doing so how corrupt one can become.

There is no harm in possessing riches, so long as the riches do not possess you. Jesus recommended that we not stockpile our treasures in this life, at the expense of accumulating our treasures for the hereafter. In other words, if one is a long-term planner and visionary, it makes much more sense to accumulate wealth for the long haul in eternity. Time here on earth is the short haul, the temporary vapor of life. Life in eternity—life in heaven—is the long-term commitment.

You own nothing and God owns everything. Whatever you have, God allowed you to accumulate. But when you die, how much of your money will you leave behind? All of it! When you die, how much of your money will you take with you? None of it! Ultimately, you don't own anything. You won't take your new BMW with you. You can't take diamond rings and precious jewelry with you. Neither can you take your house. You won't take any of the possessions you have managed to accumulate here on earth. You won't even take your body, because you don't even own it. When your spirit leaves your body, it will return to dust.

God gives you the ability earn. Your heavenly Father allows you to possess certain things, but mere possession is not ownership. Those things that you possess can be taken from you in an instant. The scores of dishonest accounting firms and corrupt corporate CEO's of our day have seen to that. Billions of honest dollars invested by millions of wage earners have disappeared.

Wage earners have seen their retirement savings disappear in a matter of mere months. You can possess, but it is God who owns. You may earn a living, but God is the one who gives you the power to get wealth.

Let's note what scriptures say about just how much you really own.

> *But remember the LORD your God, for it is he who gives you the ability to produce wealth…" (Deuteronomy 8:18)*

> *"The earth is the LORD's, and everything in it, the world, and all who live in it" (Psalms 24:1).*

> *"For every animal of the forest is mine, and the cattle on a thousand hills. I know every bird in the mountains, and the creatures of the field are mine" (Psalms 50:10,11).*

> *"Know that the LORD is God. It is he who made us, and we are his; we are his people, the sheep of his pasture" (Psalms 100:3).*

> *"For every living soul belongs to me" (Ezekiel 18:4)*

> *"'The silver is mine and the gold is mine,' declares the LORD Almighty" (Haggai 2:8).*

> *"For in him we live and move and have our being" (Acts 17:28).*

> *"Therefore, I urge you, brothers, in view of God's mercy, to offer your bodies as living sacrifices, holy and pleasing to God" (Romans 12:1).*

Because we are not our own, we should dedicate to God all that we are, all that we own, and all that we will ever be. You are God's, so all you have belongs to God. You simply manage your possessions for Him. Your life belongs to God. When everything you have belongs to God, it takes all of the pressure off you.

> *"You are not your own; you were bought at a price. Therefore honor God with your body" (I Corinthians 6:19-20).*

Let's say you are a farmer and your farm belongs to God. If the weather is dry and it doesn't rain, you don't have to worry about it because it belongs to God. If your business is dedicated to God, it becomes His problem and not yours.

The apostle Paul realized that although everything in the universe belongs to God, if we team up with Him, He allows us to keep some of everything that he brings about. Paul said the soldiers in the army do not pay for their own expenses. The farmer who harvests the crop has a right to eat some of it. The one who plants the vineyard gets to enjoy some of its fruit.

In business when you associate with God, He not only will bless it, He will let you enjoy prosperity also. But there is a caution not to keep everything to yourself. Instead of trying to figure out how little we can give to God, try giving it all to Him and ask Him how much you should keep.

*"Will a man rob God? Yet you rob me. But you ask, 'How do we rob you?' In tithes and offerings. You are under a curse— the whole nation of you— because you are robbing me. Bring the whole tithe into the storehouse, that there may be food in my house. Test me in this," says the LORD Almighty, "and see if I will not throw open the floodgates of heaven and pour out so much blessing that you will not have room enough for it. I will prevent pests from devouring your crops... "* (Malachi 3:8-11)

> *"One man gives freely, yet grows all the richer; another withholds what he should give, and only suffers want. A liberal man will be enriched, and one who waters will himself be watered" (Proverbs 11:24 RSV).*

> *"Don't be deceived, my dear brothers. Every good and perfect gift is from above, coming down from the Father..." (James 1:16,17)*

When you understand who really owns everything, then you won't have trouble trying to benefit yourself with possessions. You will begin to bless others.

When you collaborate with God, He will prosper you! When God becomes your source, then your well will never run dry. When we become Christian, we become children of God. And the Bible says that God wants to give good gifts to His children.

But God also wants to be sure that we are more interested in pleasing Him than pleasing ourselves. God is interested in your motives. Can you be trusted with prosperity? Jesus said in Matthew 6:33, "Seek ye first the kingdom of God, and his righteousness; and all these things shall be added unto you."

Our motives and priorities must be God first, me last. Sometimes we get jealous of the success of others who are not Christians. They seem to be happy and rich, while enjoying a life of luxury.

A musician and prophet in Old Testament times by the name of Asaph, said, "I was envious at the foolish, when I saw the prosperity of the wicked" (Psalms 73:3). There are ungodly men and women who may achieve material prosperity apart from God. But they can never achieve the deep settled peace that comes from God. Riches gained without God are a snare and do not bring peace. But prosperity which comes from God brings not only an abundance of possessions, but also emotional peace, happiness and great joy.

Do you know why some very wicked people are rich today? The Bible gives us a very simple explanation. The wicked who are rich are simply holding the wealth that someday God will give to His children.

> *"And the wealth of the sinner is laid up for the righteous" (Proverbs 13:22 ASV).*

> *"And my God shall supply all your need according to His riches..." (Philippians 4:19 NKJ)*

Don't make the mistake of thinking that your profession or your business is what provides your income. God is the source of your abundant supply. Jobs disappear, businesses fail; even large companies cease to exist. It is God who sees to it that your needs are being met.

Giving is the trigger for God's financial miracles. When you give to the Kingdom of God, it will be given back to you. But where will it come from? Who will give to you? Will God cause money to float down from heaven so that your needs will be met? No. The Bible says, "shall men give into your ....(life)." This is how the cycle of blessing works. When you give to God, He in turn causes others to give to you. Perhaps it will be in the form of new customers to your business, new products to sell, and so on. When God owns your business, He will make sure it prospers!

*"Give, and it shall be given unto you" (Luke 6:38).*

Nothing happens in the economy of God until you give something away. Everyone and everything else is just His instrument for getting it accomplished. God uses many vehicles to get the job done, but in the end, it is not us, but God's blessing upon our lives. It is a universal law of God. Paul very appropriately reminds us: "Remember this: Whoever sows sparingly will also reap sparingly, and whoever sows generously will also reap generously" (II Corinthians 9:6).

Jesus said in Luke 12:15, "Watch out! Be on your guard against all kinds of greed; a man's life does not consist in the abundance of his possessions." Does this mean that Christians should all be poor? No! Abraham, Isaac, Jacob, Joseph, David, Solomon, Daniel, Joseph of Arimathea, and Cornelius were all rich. Some of them were extremely wealthy. Yet each one was totally devoted to God. This means that there must be priorities in our life.

First of all, God must be recognized as the source of all things. Second, He must be credited with full ownership of all we possess. Third, it must be known that our spiritual prosperity is infinitely more important than our material prosperity.

*"Beloved, I pray that you may prosper in all things and be in health, just as your soul prospers" (III John 2 NKJ).*

A passage of Scripture in the Bible describes the reign of King Uzziah over the land of Judah. It gives us a clear guideline for today. II Chronicles 26:5 says, "As long as he sought the LORD, God gave him success". Another Scripture in the Bible tells us how to be prosperous and successful.

*"Do not let this Book of the Law depart from your mouth; meditate on it day and night, so that you may be careful to*

> *do everything written in it. Then you will be prosperous and successful" (Joshua 1:8).*

> *Give, and it will be given to you. A good measure, pressed down, shaken together and running over, will be poured into your lap. For with the measure you use, it will be measured to you. (Luke 6:38)*

Note that selflessness is the theme of this scripture. In short, the principle of enlarged measure is this. We must give if we ever hope to have a return. Secondly, the size of our return is dependent upon the size of our gift. Thirdly, our return will be bountiful; over and above our expectations.

In short, when I hoard my money and keep it all to myself, that's all I have. It never increases, but there is a huge opportunity for it to decrease. However when I give it away, God multiplies it.

Some people want to tell God that they expect Him to not only meet their needs, but to also supply them with their wants. And only then will they consider giving something away. But I am so sorry, it does not work that way. God's way is that you give first, and then he pours out the blessing. And not only that, the measure of blessing is dependent upon the measure of your gift.

## *Money CAN Buy Happiness*

Let me give you a possible scenario for buying personal happiness. What if your total income was $50,000 per year. And let's agree that you are by now a faithful and obedient tithe payer; i.e. you give God 10% of your increase and you have become a good steward of the 90% God has entrusted you with.

Obviously if you are a good manager you are already living comfortably below the 90% remainder. Now let's suppose that you work for someone else and you receive a $5,000 raise in your annual income. What should you do with that?

Should you buy a newer car? How about take a longer vacation. Maybe you could buy more "stuff" so that you need a bigger garage or a larger shed to store it in.

Consider the "happiness" alternative. Instead of using the money to heap new "stuff" upon yourself, why not use the additional increase to help others? Here's a few ideas for you.

**$ 5,000 Increase in Personal Income**

| | |
|---|---|
| <$ 500> | additional tithe to your local church |
| <$1,200> | support a missionary for $100 per month |
| <$ 500> | support a homeless shelter |
| <$ 300> | pay some utility bills of an unemployed person |
| <$ 500> | donate to a food program for the needy |
| <$ 500> | arrange for a poor family to enjoy a nice Christmas |
| <$1,000> | help a college student with tuition and/or books |
| <$ 400> | buy new tires for an older person on a fixed income |
| <$ 100> | give to a neighbor child to help with summer camp |
| $ 0 | Balance of Increase |

Try this one time with your increase and just see whether or not you receive more joy and happiness then you've ever experienced before. Honor the Lord with your increase; honor the Lord with your wealth.

# People Who Gave Generously

# People Who Gave Generously

### Paul White

BTD Manufacturing, Inc., a metal stamping and fabrication business was established by Paul White and Earl Rasmussen. Their goal was to have a company that would always honor its greatest assets; its people. Along with that was a commitment to charitable giving. The BTD Manufacturing Foundation was begun in the year 1988. The company's goal is to share the profits with people in need.

A few years ago, Paul White also established his own donor-advised family fund named the White Family Foundation. The family's charitable interests are driven in large part by a belief that people of wealth are merely stewards of those dollars on behalf of God. He says, "God gave each of us specific gifts and talents. If we use these talents in earning dollars, then we need to share those dollars with others."

### Sir John Marks Templeton

Sir John Marks Templeton is a Rhodes scholar and a Yale graduate. Early in the 40's he began to try his hand in the art of investment. He established his first mutual fund in 1954. Using this fund, he purchased international equities long before other American investors did so.

This first fund of his proved to be very successful. A typical investment of $10,000 in the year 1954 would have grown to, without additional contributions, a whopping $3 million by the year 1992. It was in 1992 that he sold his company for more than $400 million.

Mr. Templeton today remains a faith-filled, religious, values-oriented Christian philanthropist. He has been known to pay professors if they would promote conservative values. He gives to universities to build character in the lives of young persons. He funds researchers who will connect faith and science.

He launched the Templeton Prize for Progress in Religion in the year 1972. The first award went to Mother Teresa, some six years *before* she won the Nobel Peace Prize. Other winners include just as famous names as Billy Graham and Chuck Colson. In 2003 he launched the *Templeton Honor Roll* which distinguished 126 universities, departments, professors and textbooks that uphold conservative and traditional educational values.

### Andrew Carnegie

Andrew Carnegie was one of the leading industrialist of America's 19th century. Building America's steel industry made him one of the greatest and riches entrepreneurs in history. But it was not always that way. He was born in Scotland, to the son of a weaver in 1835, in a city that was the center of the linen industry.

After the industrial revolution took place, the steam-powered looms put thousands of craftsman out of work. This caused his entire family to go to work selling groceries and mending shoes. Fearing future economic survival, the family borrowed enough money to travel by ship to North America. They took up residence in Pittsburgh the iron-manufacturing center of the country.

Andrew's father found work in a cotton factory and Andrew became a bobbin boy at a pay rate of $1.20 per week. From that job he went on to become a messenger boy in the local telegraph office. Later he began working at the Pennsylvania Railroad as a private secretary and personal telegrapher for a salary of around $35 per month. He once said, "I couldn't imagine what I could ever do with so much money." Excelling in his responsibilities, he soon became the superintendent of the Pittsburgh Division. During the Civil War he helped to supervise military transportation for the North. After the war he worked for the Keystone Bridge Company replacing wooden bridges with bridges built of iron. He began earning an annual income of $50,000.

Over the ensuing years he worked to convert iron to steel, using his own personal money and borrowing additional funds to build a new steel plant near Pittsburgh. His motto was, "watch costs and the profits take care of themselves". By 1900 his plant produced more steel than all plants in Great Britain. Financier J.P. Morgan sought to take over the Carnegie Steel Company and did so at a cost of $480 million, making Andrew Carnegie the richest man in the world.

In his book, *The Gospel of Wealth*, Andrew Carnegie talks about how change has come to this nation. He states, "The poor enjoy what the rich could not before afford. What were the luxuries have become the necessaries of life.

The laborer has now more comforts than the farmer had a few generations ago. The farmer has more luxuries than the landlord had, and is more richly clad and better housed. The landlord has books and pictures rarer and appointments more artistic than the king could then obtain". He wrote this in the year 1889. I wonder what he would write today.

After spending a lifetime accumulating wealth and fortune, his later years were spent in giving it away to institutions of science, education, charitable foundations, libraries, churches and culture. By the time of his death, he had donated approximately $350 million to various worthy causes. He often said, "The man who dies rich, dies disgraced". He used his money to help others help themselves.

### Myrna Rose Strand

Myrna Strand is a retired school teacher from Minneapolis who decided to give her estate to charitable causes. She says, "My estate will never be large enough to be able to build libraries, but it may be large enough to buy some books for a library." As a young girl, she was taught and willingly placed coins in the Sunday school offering envelope each week.

Throughout her life she has been generous with her money and her time, volunteering thousands of charitable hours to church and other charities. She continues, "I have always wanted the balance of my estate to go to charities. I believe in the idea that when you come into the world you come in with nothing, and you have an obligation to give back. You can't take it with you. I believe I should carefully manage the resources God has entrusted to me, to care for his world, his people, his creation and myself."

**Martha Berry**

The Boys Industrial School was begun on land Martha Berry deeded for that purpose. As founder of the Lavender Mountain school in Georgia, she was an educator who began teaching poor children before public schools were common. Using her own personal money to fund teachers and the educational budget, the school grew quickly and the quality of student education became well known even to presidents.

In future years other schools were opened that accepted girls as well. The Berry Schools accomplished so much that she founded Berry College in 1926. Martha Berry shared her time, money and gave her life so that poor children could be educated. Her life was one of focus and attaining great goals. A devout Christian, she believed that prayer combined with personal sacrifice and generous giving could accomplish much.

**Bill & Vonette Bright**

Founders of Campus Crusade for Christ, a ministry dedicated to sharing the gospel with every person on the planet, Bill and Vonette Bright have lived a life of service to Christ. After giving his heart to God, in 1951 he received a vision to begin evangelism on college campuses worldwide.

Campus Crusade has grown to over 26,000 full-time staff members and more than 500,000 volunteers. Campus Crusade is active in 191 countries. Today Campus Crusade is the largest evangelical organization in the USA. The JESUS film was originated, distributed and translated into 800 languages.

The prestigious Templeton Prize for Progress in Religion was awarded to them in 1996. Instead of using the prize reward for personal enjoyment, they used the $1.1 million dollars to promote the spiritual discipline of fasting. With a 2001 annual ministry budget of $437 million, Bill and Vonette Bright's combined income in 2002 was $50,570.

Even though Bill Bright has written more than 60 books, all royalties have been given by him to Campus Crusade. Additionally, he has never accepted any speaking fees or honorariums. During his lifetime he gave away millions of dollars of personal income so that the world could be reached for Christ.

**William Colgate**

William C. Colgate was born in 1783, the eldest of five brothers. He came to America at the age of 12 with his father. In 1849, at the age of 16, William left home carrying his meager possessions. Meeting an old canal-boat captain, he told the old man how his father was too poor to support him anymore and that the only trade he was familiar with was that of making of soap and candles.

Kneeling, the old man prayed for the boy and then told him that someone would become the leading soap-maker in New York and it might as well be him. He urged William to give his heart to Christ. He instructed the young man on how to make a good quality of soap and give a full honest pound. He said that if he did so, he would become a prosperous and rich man.

Going into the city William united with a church. He became employed in a business, and soon became a partner and later sole owner of the business. Tithing on the very first $1 dollar he made, he continued to give to the Lord.

He instructed his bookkeeper to open a separate account with the Lord's money. As the business prospered and grew, he soon began to tithe 20%, 30%, 50% and finally gave all of his income to the Lord. Eventually he gave millions to the Lord's work around the world.

During his lifetime he organized several Bible societies including the American Bible Society in 1816 and gave generously to a New York institution of higher learning later called Colgate University.

### Henry P. Crowell

Founder of the Quaker Oats Company, and one who packaged and branded oatmeal into a worldwide brand, Henry Crowell built the company into a 250 million dollar business. As a Chicago businessman, it is said that over a period of 40 years, he gave away 70 percent of his earnings to church and charity. During his lifetime he led many business acquaintances to Christ.

### Katharine Drexel

Saint Katharine Drexel was born in 1858 the daughter of wealthy railroad businesspersons. Katherine was the second daughter of Francis Anthony and Hannah Langstroth Drexel. One month after her birth, her mother passed away. It is said that she was taught from a very early age to use her assets and benefit others in need.

Growing up, her family shared their home with the poor several days a week. In 1891, Katherine founded the Sisters of the Blessed Sacrament and later founded many other ministries. Over the years she used her wealth to found and staff many schools for both Black and Native Americans, including Xavier University. Her older sister Elizabeth founded a trade school for orphans in Pennsylvania.

A younger sister founded a liberal arts and vocational school for poor blacks in Virginia. Over her lifetime, Katharine gave systemic aid to Indian missions, spending millions of her family fortune to help them. Donating over $20 million of her own money she began black Catholic schools in 13 states, 40 mission centers, 23 rural schools, 50 Indian missions, and Xavier University in New Orleans, Louisiana.

### Jack Eckerd

The founder in 1952 of one of the largest drug store chains in the world, Jack Eckerd was a devout Christian who took his fortune and invested it in numerous charities. He funded a private college later becoming known as Eckerd College. Eckerd Youth Alternatives, which he began as a network of wilderness camps for at-risk youth, now operates 39 residential and community programs in 7 states. More than 65,000 youth have been through the program. Nearly $65 million in funding each year comes from the Eckerd Foundation.

## Francis of Assisi

St. Francis of Assisi, founder of the Franciscan Order, was born in 1182 in Assisi in Umbria. He father was Pietro Bernardone, a rich cloth merchant. Born into Italian wealth, he found joy solely in seeking after God. Desiring to live a life of devotion without the hindrances of money, he gave it all away and spent his life befriending the poor and sick.

## Selina Hastings

Countess of Huntington, born in 1707 of noble birth, Selina Hastings was a English religious leader and founder of a sect of Calvinistic Methodists. During her adult life she worked closely with John Wesley and George Whitefield in the great revival. Using her wealth she built 64 chapels in different areas of England and Wales including Bath, Brighton and London. She converted a mansion in South Wales into a theological seminary for young ministers.

## Albert Hyde

Born in 1848, Albert Hyde became a banking clerk for several years. After that he devoted his time to the booming real estate market. When that bubble burst, he entered into a business partnership and created the Yucca Company which later became the Mentholatum Company. This company manufactured and sold toilet soap. Its success depended heavily upon doctors, chemists, good salesmanship, word-of-mouth, and the favor of the druggists.

In search of new products to produce, and intrigues with the properties of menthol, Hyde developed a product know today as Mentholatum, known to cure many ills. The name of Mentholatum came to be linked solely with that of A. Hyde. Other products included fly paper, cough syrup and silver polish.

Becoming a man of great wealth because of its success, Albert Hyde decided to give all of his money away during his lifetime. He gave multiplied millions to the Y.M.C.A. At one time all of his Japan profits from his products was used to support missionary work there. When he died he had given millions to missions. At the time of his death in 1935 he died without accumulated wealth, thus fulfilling his lifetime wish.

### Robert A. Laidlaw

Born in 1885 in Scotland, Robert Laidlaw became one of New Zealand's most successful businessmen. He was a self-made millionaire who's first business venture was a mail order company named Laidlaw Leeds. This business was consolidated with the Farmers Union Trading Company in 1918. In 1919 he bought his first 12-store chain and by 1933 there were some 60 branches; business was booming.

Early in his business life he began giving ten percent of his income. He started tithing at the age of eighteen on his weekly salary of just $3. This 10% soon went to 15%, then to 20% and later to 25%. At the age of twenty-five he wrote in his journal, "I have decided to change my earlier graduated scale, and start now giving fifty percent of all my earnings." For the next sixty years he did just that.

He played a major role in establishing several Christian initiatives in New Zealand. After World War II he retired from the activities of regular business and devoted his time largely to church involvement and Christian missionary work.

### Robert G. LeTourneau

Born in 1888 to godly parents, accepting Christ as Savior at age 16, Robert LeTourneau dedicated his business life to God at age 30. He dropped out of school at age fourteen and went to work shoveling sand and dirt at an iron works factory in Portland, Oregon. Working around men of the world, his heart became hardened toward God.

Just before Christmas in 1904, the city of Portland had a Gospel crusade and LeTourneau decide to attend. After singing hymns and listening to sermons he didn't feel any conviction leading to a quick response. That concerned him so much that he knew he needed to pray for salvation. After doing so, he became aware of a Divine Presence in his life.

He was a designer and builder of earthmoving equipment. He pioneered the welding of various metals, built huge mobile offshore drilling platforms and brought new technology to the earthmoving and material handling industry. During his lifetime his company designed and built some of the world's most massive machinery including bridge building equipment, drilling rigs, missile launchers and earth movers. He was an internationally recognized industrialist.

In his manufacturing plants he employed three full-time Chaplains. He traveled the world sharing the Gospel with other businesspersons. He established missionary ministries in the countries of Liberia, West Africa, Peru and other South American countries. He and his wife founded LeTourneau University. He took no credit for personal success and wealth, but always gave credit to God; saying often, "I'm just a mechanic that God has blessed…".

For most of his successful life, he lived on ten percent of his income and gave ninety percent to Christian work. "The question", he said, "is not how much of my money I give to God, but rather how much of God's money I keep for myself."

## Jiang Minde

Born in a mountain village in 1946, Jiang Minde searched for God and found the Christian faith. In 1984 he began to produce a food for child nutrition called "Future." His annual production has reached 8,000 tons of rice noodles. Although a wealthy man, he chooses to live a simple lifestyle, living in an ordinary house.

He states, "My money comes from God, it was given to me by God for safeguarding. Hence, I cannot spend it recklessly, but ought to help those in need. As long as I have enough to eat and for my own needs, it is sufficient." Yet when it comes to meeting the many needs of those in poverty, Jaing Minde is very generous. Since 1985 he has given more than $1.69 million to charity. Jiang says this; "With my work, I want to genuinely represent the Christian spirit of love to our neighbor."

### George Muller

Born in Prussia in 1805, the son of a revenue collector, George Muller spent childhood money foolishly, stole government money while his father was out and wandered into great sin. At ten years of age, his father sent him away to a cathedral school to be trained in the ways of a Lutheran clergyman.

During this time he engaged in sinful practices; lying, cheating, gambling, gross immorality, and often spent his evenings in the taverns, then wandering the streets during early morning hours after becoming intoxicated with strong drink. This lifestyle led to imprisonment at the age of sixteen.

After attending some Christian Bible studies in a friend's home, in time he sobered up, got married and begin to lead an exemplanary life. Muller began preaching in many towns and cities, winning many to Christ. He eventually became co-pastor at Gideon and Bethesda Chapels in Bristol, in 1832. The congregations grew and at the time of his death he had a congregation of about two thousand persons at Bethesda Chapel.

George Mueller also started a very large orphanage and became a man of great faith. His efforts to operate an institution that cared for the daily needs of destitute children, required great faith and trust in God as a daily provider.

One night before going to bed his staff informed him that there was absolutely no food in the building for the children's breakfast in the morning. He told them to go ahead and set the table for the morning meal and then he went to pray.

Early the next morning, there came a knock on the door. A local baker was awakened during the night with an overpowering feeling that he must get up and bake bread for the children. A few minutes later another knock on the orphanage door.

The local dairyman's delivery cart had broken down in the neighborhood. Knowing that the milk would spoil before the cart could be repaired, he asked Mueller if he would take the milk off his hands. Of course the children never went hungry...not even for a single day.

In addition to the orphanages, Muller started the Scripture Knowledge Institution for Home and Abroad. Its purpose was to aid Christian schools, assist missionaries, and to circulate the Scriptures.

At the time of his death 282,000 Bibles and 1,500,000 Testaments had been distributed and 112,000,000 religious books, pamphlets and tracts had been circulated. At the age of seventy, George Muller began a trek of evangelistic tours. Traveling over 200,000 miles and around the world he spoke to thousands of people. He continued traveling until the age of ninety.

A man who built great orphanages in England, did so with a vision from God and 50 cents in his pocket. He never made his needs known to man, praying only to God. Over $7 million was sent to him for ministry including the building and the maintaining of these orphan homes. At the time of his death, these five immense homes for orphans housed more than two thousand orphans.

After spending his last 17 years speaking to the nations, he died at the age of 93, leaving an estate valued at less than one thousand dollars. Yet he had given the Institute almost one-half million dollars of personal honorariums he had received during his ministry.

### Saint Nicholas

Nicholas, born in Patara which is now Turkey, was the son of wealthy parents who raised him to be a devout Christian. Taking the words of Jesus literally when he told the rich young ruler to "sell what you own and give the money to the poor," Nicholas did just that. He took his entire inheritance and assisted the needy, the sick and those who were suffering.

After dedicating is life to serving God, in time he was made the Bishop of Myra, becoming known as one who gave generously to people in need as well as his love for children and his concern for sailors. He was persecuted for his faith by the Roman Emperor Diocletian and subsequently exiled and imprisoned. Upon release he attended the Council of Nicaea in 325 AD.

### James Cash Penney

This man's name became associated with doing business according to the Golden Rule. Born in 1875 into a poor farm family, he was a boy with plenty of self-discipline, very self- reliant and much personal character.

Having to purchase his own clothing at the age of eight and needing a pair of shoes, he saved $2.50 earned from running errands, selling junk and performing any farm tasks available to him. He began to invest his earnings by buying and selling pigs, raising watermelons, horse trading and very quickly learned the ways of an entrepreneur.

His post high school career included clerking at a local dry goods store and investing in a butcher shop. Because he would not provide the chef of the local hotel with a weekly bottle of bourbon, he lost his biggest account and the butcher business soon failed. After that he went to work for the Golden Rule Stores and soon became a business partner in one of their new stores in Wyoming.

Before opening the store he studied the town and their needs, stocked the shelves with quality merchandise. It was an instant success. In subsequent years, James Cash Penney purchased all of the stores and opened more. In all of his stores he insisted on offering the lowest possible prices on the very best merchandise. At the end of 1912 he had opened 34 stores with sales in excess of $2 million.

In the 1920s there were 197 J.C. Penney stores with sales of nearly $43 million. At age ninety, J.C. Penney maintained a full schedule of appointments and at the age of 95 still traveled to his 45$^{th}$ floor office and worked three days each week.

In 1911, Mr. Penney donated $10,000 to the First Methodist Church in Salt Lake City. In 1923 he established a 120,000 acre experimental farming community in northern Florida. This was divided into small plots where industries and moral, but economically destitute farmers could live and work and rebuild their lives.

In 1925 he established the J.C. Penney Foundation which funded such ministries as adoption agencies, homeless shelters, youth clubs, vocational libraries, family guidance centers, missionary projects, peace organizations and health clinics.

Next to this he established the Memorial Home Community which is a 60 acre residential community for retired ministers, lay church workers, missionaries, their wives and families. In later years he donated to many other organizations including the National 4-H clubs, Junior Achievement and other community needs.

## John D. Rockefeller

Born in 1839 in New York, John Rockefeller had a mother who was very religious and very disciplined. She taught him to work hard, save much and become a generous giver to charities. At age 12 he had saved $50 working for neighbors and raising turkeys. At the age of 16 he became an assistant bookkeeper with a merchant and produce shipper. At the age of 20 he went into business with a neighbor to form a company that traded in grain, hay, meats and other goods. From there it was the oil refining business and then the creation of the Standard Oil Company of Ohio.

From the mid 1890s until his death in 1937, Mr. Rockefeller was consumed with philanthropic activity. His fortune had peaked in 1912 at nearly $900 million. He began to give away hundreds of millions of dollars. Largely responsible for creating the University of Chicago, he pitched in a mere $75 million in 1932.

Also in the 1930s he set up the Rockefeller Institute for medical research and his gifts totaled $50 million. He gave more than $530 million to various educational, scientific and religious institutions. This included gifts to Baptist institutions, the Y.M.C.A., Anti-Saloon League and colleges.

When asked about his giving his response was, "Yes, I tithe, and I would like to tell you how it all came about. I had to begin work as a small boy to help support my mother. My first wages amounted to $1.50 per week. The first week after I went to work, I took the $1.50 home to my mother and she held the money in her lap and explained to me that she would be happy if I would give a tenth of it to the Lord.

I did, and from that week until this day I have tithed every dollar God has entrusted to me. And I want to say, if I had not tithed the first dollar I made I would not have tithed the first million dollars I made. Tell your readers to train the children to tithe, and they will grow up to be faithful stewards of the Lord. "

John D. Rockefeller once said, "Every right implies a responsibility; Every opportunity, an obligation, Every possession, a duty."

### Stanley Tam

At the early age of twenty, Stanley Tam began a silver recovery business that built collectors into tanks that photographers, X-ray labs and printers could use to retrieve the silver. It was 1936 and Tam was soon broke. He told the Lord that if God would take the business and make it succeed, that Tam would honor Him in every way He possible could.

Four years later as the business grew, Tam decided he needed a senior partner. Going to a lawyer who thought he must be crazy, an agreement was finally drawn up with God as partner. He put into writing that 51% of the profits would go to missionary and church work. In the ensuing years, the business flourished. He soon began giving 60% of his income to missionary work.

On January 15, 1955 he told God that he would turn the entire business over to him and that he would no longer even be a stockholder in the company. Founding additional companies, Stanley Tam continued the giving.

The United States Plastic Corporation established more than 50 years ago by Mr. Tam in Lima, Ohio, was also placed under the ownership of God. Stanley Tam placed 100% of the stock ownership into a foundation whose purpose is to establish churches in third world countries.

# Appendix A:

# Biblical References on Success: Its Integrity, Function, & Process

## Author of Ecclesiastes

**Ecclesiastes 9:10**

> *Whatever your hand finds to do, verily, do {it} with all your might; for there is no activity or planning or knowledge or wisdom in Sheol where you are going. (NAS)*

## David

**Psalms 112:5**

> *...and all goes well for the generous man who conducts his business fairly. (TLB)*

**1 Samuel 21:8**

> *David asked Ahimelech if he had a spear or sword he could use. "The king's business required such haste, and I left in such a rush that I came away without a weapon!" David explained. (TLB)*

**1 Chronicles 28:20**

*And David said to Solomon his son, Be strong and of good courage, and do it: fear not, nor be dismayed: for the LORD God, even my God, will be with thee; he will not fail thee, nor forsake thee, until thou hast finished all the work for the service of the house of the LORD. (KJV)*

## God

**Exodus 20:15**

*Thou shalt not steal. (KJV)*

**Exodus 20:16**

*You must not lie. (TLB)*

## Isaiah

**Isaiah 33:15-16**

*I will tell you who can live here: All who are honest and fair, who reject making profit by fraud, who hold back their hands from taking bribes, who refuse to listen to those who plot murder, who shut their eyes to all enticement to do wrong. Such as these shall dwell on high. The rocks of the mountains will be their fortress of safety; food will be supplied to them, and they will have all the water they need. (TLB)*

## Jesus Christ

**Matthew 5:34-37**

*But I say: Don't make any vows! And even to say 'By heavens!' is a sacred vow to God, for the heavens are God's throne. And if you say 'By the earth!' it is a sacred vow, for the earth is his footstool. And don't swear 'By Jerusalem!' for Jerusalem is the capital of the great King. Don't even swear 'By my head!' for you can't turn one hair white or black. Say just a simple 'Yes, I will' or 'No, I won't.' Your word is enough. To strengthen your promise with a vow shows that something is wrong. (TLB)*

**Mark 8:36**

*And how does a man benefit if he gains the whole world and loses his soul in the process? (TLB)*

**Luke 2:49**

*And He said to them, "Why did you seek Me? Did you not know that I must be about My Father's business?" (NKJ)*

**John 9:4**

*All of us must quickly carry out the tasks assigned us by the one who sent me, for there is little time left before the night falls and all work comes to an end. (TLB)*

## John The Baptist

**Luke 3:13-14**

*"By your honesty," he replied. "Make sure you collect no more taxes than the Roman government requires you to." "And us," asked some soldiers, "what about us?" John replied, "Don't extort money by threats and violence; don't accuse anyone of what you know he didn't do; and be content with your pay!"*

(TLB)

## Joshua

**Joshua 1:6**

*"Be strong and brave, for you will be a successful leader of my people; and they shall conquer all the land I promised to their ancestors. (TLB)*

**Ezekiel 45:10**

*You must use honest scales, honest bushels, honest gallons. (TLB)*

## Moses

Exodus 23:12

*"Six days you shall do your work, and on the seventh day you shall rest, that your ox and your donkey may rest, and*

*the son of your female servant and the stranger may be refreshed.(NKJ)*

## Paul

### Romans 12:11

*Not slothful in business; fervent in spirit; serving the Lord; (KJV)*

### 1 Thessalonians 4:6

*...and that in this matter no one should wrong his brother or take advantage of him. The Lord will punish men for all such sins, as we have already told you and warned you.*

### 1Thessalonians 4:11

*And that ye study to be quiet, and to do your own business, and to work with your own hands, as we commanded you; (KJV)*

### Romans13:7

*Pay all of them their dues, taxes to whom taxes are due, revenue to whom revenue is due, respect to whom respect is due, honor to whom honor is due.*(RSV)

**2 Thessalonians 3:10**

*For even when we were with you, we commanded you this: If anyone will not work, neither shall he eat. (NKJ)*

## Solomon

**Proverbs 22:29**

*Seest thou a man diligent in his business? he shall stand before kings; he shall not stand before mean men.*

## Success Work Ethic

**Ecclesiastes 9:10**

*Whatever your hand finds to do, do it with all your might, for in the grave, where you are going, there is neither working nor planning nor knowledge nor wisdom.*

**Proverbs14:23**

*All hard work brings a profit, but mere talk leads only to poverty.*

**Proverbs 27:18**

*He who tends a fig tree will eat its fruit, and he who looks after his master will be honored.*

**Luke 19:15**

*He was made king, however, and returned home. Then he sent for the servants to whom he had given the money, in order to find out what they had gained with it.*

**Matthew 22:5**

*But they paid no attention and went off-one to his field, another to his business.*

## Success & Wishful Thinking

**Proverbs 28:19**

*He who works his land will have abundant food, but the one who chases fantasies will have his fill of poverty.*

## Business Profits and Loss

**Proverbs 14:23**

*All hard work brings a profit, but mere talk leads only to poverty.*

## Honesty in Business Transactions

**Proverbs 11:1**

*The LORD abhors dishonest scales, but accurate weights are his delight.*

**Proverbs 20:10**

*Differing weights and differing measures—the LORD detests them both.*

**Deuteronomy 25:15-16**

*You must have accurate and honest weights and measures, so that you may live long in the land the LORD your God is giving you. 16 For the LORD your God detests anyone who does these things, anyone who deals dishonestly.*

**Luke 6:38**

*Give, and it will be given to you. A good measure, pressed down, shaken together and running over, will be poured into your lap. For with the measure you use, it will be measured to you."*

## Success & Wealth

**Proverbs 13:7**

*One man pretends to be rich, yet has nothing; another pretends to be poor, yet has great wealth.*

**Psalms 49:16-17**

*Do not be overawed when a man grows rich, when the splendor of his house increases; for he will take nothing with him when he dies, his splendor will not descend with him.*

**Matthew 6:20**

*But store up for yourselves treasures in heaven, where moth and rust do not destroy, and where thieves do not break in and steal.*

**Proverbs 27:24**

*For riches do not endure forever, and a crown is not secure for all generations.*

**Proverbs 23:5**

*Cast but a glance at riches, and they are gone, for they will surely sprout wings and fly off to the sky like an eagle.*

**Deuteronomy 8:18**

*But remember the LORD your God, for it is he who gives you the ability to produce wealth, and so confirms his covenant, which he swore to your forefathers, as it is today.*

**Psalms 49:10**

*For all can see that wise men die; the foolish and the senseless alike perish and leave their wealth to others.*

## Wish Granted a Successful Businessman

### 2 Chronicles 1:7-12

*That night God appeared to Solomon and said to him, "Ask for whatever you want me to give you." Solomon answered God, "You have shown great kindness to David my father and have made me king in his place. Now, LORD God, let your promise to my father David be confirmed, for you have made me king over a people who are as numerous as the dust of the earth. Give me wisdom and knowledge, that I may lead this people, for who is able to govern this great people of yours?" God said to Solomon, "Since this is your heart's desire and you have not asked for wealth, riches or honor, nor for the death of your enemies, and since you have not asked for a long life but for wisdom and knowledge to govern my people over whom I have made you king, therefore wisdom and knowledge will be given you. And I will also give you wealth, riches and honor, such as no king who was before you ever had and none after you will have."*

## Wish Refused a Successful Businessman

### Luke 16:19-31

*There was a rich man who was dressed in purple and fine linen and lived in luxury every day. At his gate was laid a beggar named Lazarus, covered with sores and longing to eat what fell from the rich man's table. Even the dogs came and licked his sores. "The time came when the beg-*

*gar died and the angels carried him to Abraham's side. The rich man also died and was buried. In hell, where he was in torment, he looked up and saw Abraham far away, with Lazarus by his side. So he called to him, 'Father Abraham, have pity on me and send Lazarus to dip the tip of his finger in water and cool my tongue, because I am in agony in this fire.' "But Abraham replied, 'Son, remember that in your lifetime you received your good things, while Lazarus received bad things, but now he is comforted here and you are in agony. And besides all this, between us and you a great chasm has been fixed, so that those who want to go from here to you cannot, nor can anyone cross over from there to us.' "He answered, 'Then I beg you, father, send Lazarus to my father's house, for I have five brothers. Let him warn them, so that they will not also come to this place of torment.' "Abraham replied, 'They have Moses and the Prophets; let them listen to them.' "'No, father Abraham,' he said, 'but if someone from the dead goes to them, they will repent.' "He said to him, 'If they do not listen to Moses and the Prophets, they will not be convinced even if someone rises from the dead.'"*

## Success & Wealth Tested

### Genesis 22:1-13

*Some time later God tested Abraham. He said to him, "Abraham!" "Here I am," he replied. Then God said, "Take your son, your only son, Isaac, whom you love, and go to the region of Moriah. Sacrifice him there as a burnt offering on one of the mountains I will tell you about." Early the next morning Abraham got up and saddled his donkey. He took with him two of his servants and his son Isaac. When he had cut enough wood for the burnt offering, he set out for the place God had told him about. On the third day Abraham looked up and saw the place in the distance. He said to his servants, "Stay here with the donkey while I and the boy go over there. We will worship and then we will come back to you." Abraham took the wood for the burnt offering and placed it on his son Isaac, and he himself carried the fire and the knife. As the two of them went on together, Isaac spoke up and said to his father Abraham, "Father?" "Yes, my son?" Abraham replied. "The fire and wood are here," Isaac said, "but where is the lamb for the burnt offering?" Abraham answered, "God himself will provide the lamb for the burnt offering, my son." And the two of them went on together. When they reached the place God had told him about, Abraham built an altar there and arranged the wood on it. He bound his son Isaac and laid him on the altar, on top of the wood. Then he reached out his hand and took the knife to slay his son. But the angel of the LORD called out to him from heaven, "Abraham! Abraham!" "Here I am," he replied. "Do not lay a hand on the boy," he said. "Do not do anything to him. Now I know that you fear God, because you have not withheld from me your son, your only son." Abraham looked up and there in a thicket he saw a ram caught by its horns. He went over and took the ram and sacrificed it as a burnt offering instead of his son.*

## Satan's Test

### Job 2:1-10

*On another day the angels came to present themselves before the LORD, and Satan also came with them to present himself before him. And the LORD said to Satan, "Where have you come from?" Satan answered the LORD, "From roaming through the earth and going back and forth in it." Then the LORD said to Satan, "Have you considered my servant Job? There is no one on earth like him; he is blameless and upright, a man who fears God and shuns evil. And he still maintains his integrity, though you incited me against him to ruin him without any reason." "Skin for skin!" Satan replied. "A man will give all he has for his own life. But stretch out your hand and strike his flesh and bones, and he will surely curse you to your face." The LORD said to Satan, "Very well, then, he is in your hands; but you must spare his life." So Satan went out from the presence of the LORD and afflicted Job with painful sores from the soles of his feet to the top of his head. Then Job took a piece of broken pottery and scraped himself with it as he sat among the ashes. His wife said to him, "Are you still holding on to your integrity? Curse God and die!" He replied, "You are talking like a foolish woman. Shall we accept good from God, and not trouble?" In all this, Job did not sin in what he said.*

## God's Restoration

### Job 42:10-17

*After Job had prayed for his friends, the LORD made him prosperous again and gave him twice as much as he had before. All his brothers and sisters and everyone who had known him before came and ate with him in his house. They comforted and consoled him over all the trouble the LORD had brought upon him, and each one gave him a piece of silver and a gold ring. The LORD blessed the latter part of Job's life more than the first. He had fourteen thousand sheep, six thousand camels, a thousand yoke of oxen and a thousand donkeys. And he also had seven sons and three daughters. The first daughter he named Jemimah, the second Keziah and the third Keren-Happuch. Nowhere in all the land were there found women as beautiful as Job's daughters, and their father granted them an inheritance along with their brothers. After this, Job lived a hundred and forty years; he saw his children and their children to the fourth generation. And so he died, old and full of years.*

# Success in Scripture

# Success in Scripture

## King James Version

**Joshua 1:8**

*This book of the law shall not depart out of thy mouth; but thou shalt meditate therein day and night, that thou mayest observe to do according to all that is written therein: for then thou shalt make thy way prosperous, and then thou shalt have good success . KJV*

## American Standard Version

**Joshua1:7-8**

*Only be strong and very courageous, to observe to do according to all the law, which Moses my servant commanded thee: turn not from it to the right hand or to the left, that thou mayest have good success whithersoever thou goest.*

*This book of the law shall not depart out of thy mouth, but thou shalt meditate thereon day and night, that thou may-*

*est observe to do according to all that is written therein: for then thou shalt make thy way prosperous, and then thou shalt have good success . ASV*

## Amplified Version

### Genesis 24:12

*And he said, O Lord, God of my master Abraham, I pray You, cause me to meet with good success today, and show kindness to my master Abraham. AMP*

### Joshua 1:8

*This Book of the Law shall not depart out of your mouth, but you shall meditate on it day and night, that you may observe and do according to all that is written in it. For then you shall make your way prosperous, and then you shall deal wisely and have good success. AMP*

### 1 Samuel 18:30

*Then the Philistine princes came out to battle, and when they did so, David had more success and behaved himself more wisely than all Saul's servants, so that his name was very dear and highly esteemed. AMP*

**Psalms 118:25**

*Save now, we beseech You, O Lord; send now prosperity, O Lord, we beseech You, and give to us success! AMP*

**Zechariah 8:10**

*For before those days there was no hire for man nor any hire for beast, neither was there any peace or success to him who went out or came in because of the adversary and oppressor, for I set (let loose) all men, every one against his neighbor. AMP*

**2 John 11**

For he who wishes him success [who encourages him, wishing him Godspeed] is a partaker in his evil doings. AMP

# New American Standard Bible

**Genesis 24:11-12**

*And he said, "O LORD, the God of my master Abraham, please grant me success today, and show lovingkindness to my master Abraham. NASB*

**Joshua 1:7**

*Only be strong and very courageous; be careful to do according to all the law which Moses My servant commanded you; do not turn from it to the right or to the left, so that you may have success wherever you go. NASB*

**Joshua 1:7- 8**

*This book of the law shall not depart from your mouth, but you shall meditate on it day and night, so that you may be careful to do according to all that is written in it; for then you will make your way prosperous, and then you will have success . NASB*

**Nehemiah 2:19-20**

*So I answered them and said to them, "The God of heaven will give us success ; therefore we His servants will arise and build, but you have no portion, right, or memorial in Jerusalem." NASB*

**Job 5:12**

*He frustrates the plotting of the shrewd, So that their hands cannot attain success. NASB*

**Ecclesiastes 10:9-11**

*If the axe is dull and he does not sharpen its edge, then he must exert more strength. Wisdom has the advantage of giving success. NASB*

**Daniel 6:28**

*So this Daniel enjoyed success in the reign of Darius and in the reign of Cyrus the Persian. NASB*

# New Revised Standard Version

**Genesis 24:11-13**

*And he said, "O LORD, God of my master Abraham, please grant me success today and show steadfast love to my master Abraham. NRSV*

**Genesis 27:20**

*But Isaac said to his son, "How is it that you have found it so quickly, my son?" He answered, "Because the LORD your God granted me success. NRSV*

**1 Samuel 18:14-16**

*David had success in all his undertakings; for the LORD was with him. 15 When Saul saw that he had great success , he stood in awe of him. 16 But all Israel and Judah loved David; for it was he who marched out and came in leading them. NRSV*

**1 Samuel 18:30-19:1**

*Then the commanders of the Philistines came out to battle; and as often as they came out, David had more success than all the servants of Saul, so that his fame became very great. NRSV*

**Nehemiah 1:10-11**

*O Lord, let your ear be attentive to the prayer of your servant, and to the prayer of your servants who delight in revering your name. Give success to your servant today, and grant him mercy in the sight of this man!" NRSV*

**Nehemiah 2:20**

*Then I replied to them, "The God of heaven is the one who will give us success , and we his servants are going to start building; but you have no share or claim or historic right in Jerusalem." NRSV*

**Job 5:12**

*He frustrates the devices of the crafty, so that their hands achieve no success . NRSV*

**Psalms 118:25**

*Save us, we beseech you, O LORD! O LORD, we beseech you, give us success ! NRSV*

**Isaiah 48:18-19**

*O that you had paid attention to my commandments! Then your prosperity would have been like a river, and your success like the waves of the sea; 19 your offspring would have been like the sand, and your descendants like its grains; their name would never be cut off or destroyed from before me. NRSV*

# Today's English Version

**Genesis 24:12**

*He prayed, "LORD, God of my master Abraham, give me success today and keep your promise to my master.*

**Genesis 24:21**

*The man kept watching her in silence, to see if the LORD had given him success.*

**Genesis 24:40**

*He answered, 'The LORD, whom I have always obeyed, will send his angel with you and give you success. You will get for my son a wife from my own people, from my father's family.*

**Genesis 24:42**

*"When I came to the well today, I prayed, 'LORD, God of my master Abraham, please give me success in what I am doing.*

**Genesis 24:56**

*But he said, "Don't make us stay. The LORD has made my journey a success; let me go back to my master."*

**1 Samuel 18:15**

*Saul noticed David's success and became even more afraid of him.*

**1 Kings 2:33**

*The punishment for their murders will fall on Joab and on his descendants forever. But the LORD will always give success to David's descendants who sit on his throne."*

**1 Kings 21:13**

*The two scoundrels publicly accused him of cursing God and the king, and so he was taken outside the city and stoned to death.*

**1 Chronicles 12:18**

*God's spirit took control of one of them, Amasai, who later became the commander of "The Thirty," and he called out, "David son of Jesse, we are yours! Success to you and those who help you!*

*God is on your side." David welcomed them and made them officers in his army.*

**2 Chronicles 18:12**

*Meanwhile, the official who had gone to get Micaiah said to him, "All the other prophets have prophesied success for the king, and you had better do the same."*

**Nehemiah 1:10**

*"Lord, these are your servants, your own people. You rescued them by your great power and strength.*

**Nehemiah 2:20**

*I answered, "The God of Heaven will give us success. We are his servants, and we are going to start building. But you have no right to any property in Jerusalem, and you have no share in its traditions."*

**Job 10:16**

*If I have any success at all, you hunt me down like a lion; to hurt me you even work miracles.*

**Job 20:22**

*At the height of his success all the weight of misery will crush him.*

**Psalms 35:27**

*May those who want to see me acquitted shout for joy and say again and again, "How great is the LORD! He is pleased with the success of his servant."*

**Psalms 90:17**

*LORD our God, may your blessings be with us. Give us success in all we do!*

**Psalms 118:25**

*Save us, LORD, save us! Give us success, O LORD!*

**Proverbs 8:18**

*I have riches and honor to give, prosperity and success.*

**Isaiah 48:15**

*I am the one who spoke and called him; I led him out and gave him success.*

**2 Corinthians 13:7**

*We pray to God that you will do no wrong — not in order to show that we are a success, but so that you may do what is right, even though we may seem to be failures.*

# New Living Translation

**Genesis 24:12**

*"O LORD, God of my master," he prayed. "Give me success and show kindness to my master, Abraham. Help me to accomplish the purpose of my journey.*

**Genesis 24:42**

*"So this afternoon when I came to the spring I prayed this prayer: 'O LORD, the God of my master, Abraham, if you are planning to make my mission a success, please guide me in a special way.*

**Genesis 39:3**

*Potiphar noticed this and realized that the LORD was with Joseph, giving him success in everything he did.*

**Joshua 2:22**

*The spies went up into the hill country and stayed there three days. The men who were chasing them had searched everywhere along the road, but they finally returned to the city without success.*

**2 Samuel 8:10**

*he sent his son Joram to congratulate David on his success. Hadadezer and Toi had long been enemies, and there had been many wars between them. Joram presented David with many gifts of silver, gold, and bronze.*

**2 Samuel 17:20**

*When Absalom's men arrived, they asked her, "Have you seen Ahimaaz and Jonathan?" She replied, "They were here, but they crossed the brook." Absalom's men looked for them without success and returned to Jerusalem.*

**2 Samuel 23:1**

*These are the last words of David:*
*"David, the son of Jesse, speaks —*
*David, the man to whom God gave such wonderful success,*
*David, the man anointed by the God of Jacob,*
*David, the sweet psalmist of Israel.*

**2 Samuel 23:5**

*"It is my family God has chosen! Yes, he has made an everlasting covenant with me. His agreement is eternal, final, sealed. He will constantly look after my safety and success.*

**1 Kings 22:13**

*Meanwhile, the messenger who went to get Micaiah said to him, "Look, all the prophets are promising victory for the king. Be sure that you agree with them and promise success."*

**1 Chronicles 12:18**

*Then the Spirit came upon Amasai, who later became a leader among the Thirty, and he said, "We are yours, David! We are on your side, son of Jesse. Peace and prosperity be with you, and success to all who help you, for your God is the one who helps you." So David let them join him, and he made them officers over his troops.*

**1 Chronicles 18:10**

*he sent his son Joram to congratulate David on his success. Hadadezer and Toi had long been enemies, and there had been many wars between them. Joram presented David with many gifts of gold, silver, and bronze.*

**1 Chronicles 22:11**

*"Now, my son, may the LORD be with you and give you success as you follow his instructions in building the Temple of the LORD your God.*

**2 Chronicles 18:12**

*Meanwhile, the messenger who went to get Micaiah said to him, "Look, all the prophets are promising victory for the king. Be sure that you agree with them and promise success."*

**2 Chronicles 26:5**

*Uzziah sought God during the days of Zechariah, who instructed him in the fear of God. And as long as the king sought the LORD, God gave him success.*

**Ezra 5:8**

*We wish to inform you that we went to the construction site of the Temple of the great God in the province of Judah. It is being rebuilt with specially prepared stones, and timber is being laid in its walls. The work is going forward with great energy and success.*

**Nehemiah 1:11**

*O Lord, please hear my prayer! Listen to the prayers of those of us who delight in honoring you. Please grant me success now as I go to ask the king for a great favor. Put it into his heart to be kind to me." In those days I was the king's cup-bearer.*

**Job 6:13**

*No, I am utterly helpless, without any chance of success.*

**Psalms 21:3**

*You welcomed him back with success and prosperity. You placed a crown of finest gold on his head.*

**Psalms 49:18**

*In this life they consider themselves fortunate, and the world loudly applauds their success.*

**Psalms 92:7**

*Although the wicked flourish like weeds, and evildoers blossom with success, there is only eternal destruction ahead of them.*

**Psalms 118:25**

*Please, LORD, please save us. Please, LORD, please give us success.*

**Proverbs 8:14**

*Good advice and success belong to me. Insight and strength are mine.*

**Proverbs 15:22**

*Plans go wrong for lack of advice; many counselors bring success.*

**Ecclesiastes 4:4**

*Then I observed that most people are motivated to success by their envy of their neighbors. But this, too, is meaningless, like chasing the wind.*

**Daniel 11:12**

*After the enemy army is swept away, the king of the south will be filled with pride and will have many thousands of his enemies killed. But his success will be short lived.*

**John 3:29**

*The bride will go where the bridegroom is. A bridegroom's friend rejoices with him. I am the bridegroom's friend, and I am filled with joy at his success.*

**2 Corinthians 3:5**

*It is not that we think we can do anything of lasting value by ourselves. Our only power and success come from God.*

# New International Version

**Genesis 24:12**

*Then he prayed, "O LORD, God of my master Abraham, give me success today, and show kindness to my master Abraham.*

**Genesis 24:40**

*"He replied, 'The LORD, before whom I have walked, will send his angel with you and make your journey a success, so that you can get a wife for my son from my own clan and from my father's family.*

**Genesis 24:42**

*"When I came to the spring today, I said, 'O LORD, God of my master Abraham, if you will, please grant success to the journey on which I have come.*

**Genesis 24:56**

*But he said to them, "Do not detain me, now that the LORD has granted success to my journey. Send me on my way so I may go to my master."*

**Genesis 27:20**

*Isaac asked his son, "How did you find it so quickly, my son?" "The LORD your God gave me success," he replied.*

**Genesis 39:3**

*When his master saw that the LORD was with him and that the LORD gave him success in everything he did,*

**Genesis 39:23**

*The warden paid no attention to anything under Joseph's care, because the LORD was with Joseph and gave him success in whatever he did.*

**1 Samuel 18:14**

*In everything he did he had great success, because the LORD was with him.*

**1 Samuel 18:30**

*The Philistine commanders continued to go out to battle, and as often as they did, David met with more success than the rest of Saul's officers, and his name became well known.*

**1 Samuel 25:31**

*my master will not have on his conscience the staggering burden of needless bloodshed or of having avenged himself. And when the LORD has brought my master success, remember your servant."*

**1 Kings 22:13**

*The messenger who had gone to summon Micaiah said to him, "Look, as one man the other prophets are predicting success for the king. Let your word agree with theirs, and speak favorably."*

**1 Chronicles 12:18**

*Then the Spirit came upon Amasai, chief of the Thirty, and he said: "We are yours, O David! We are with you, O son of Jesse! Success, success to you, and success to those who help you, for your God will help you." So David received them and made them leaders of his raiding bands.*

**1 Chronicles 22:11**

*"Now, my son, the LORD be with you, and may you have success and build the house of the LORD your God, as he said you would.*

**1 Chronicles 22:13**

*Then you will have success if you are careful to observe the decrees and laws that the LORD gave Moses for Israel. Be strong and courageous. Do not be afraid or discouraged.*

**2 Chronicles 18:12**

*The messenger who had gone to summon Micaiah said to him, "Look, as one man the other prophets are predicting success for the king. Let your word agree with theirs, and speak favorably."*

**2 Chronicles 26:5**

*He sought God during the days of Zechariah, who instructed him in the fear of God. As long as he sought the LORD, God gave him success.*

**Nehemiah 1:11**

*O Lord, let your ear be attentive to the prayer of this your servant and to the prayer of your servants who delight in revering your name. Give your servant success today by granting him favor in the presence of this man."*

*I was cupbearer to the king.*

**Nehemiah 2:20**

*I answered them by saying, "The God of heaven will give us success. We his servants will start rebuilding, but as for you, you have no share in Jerusalem or any claim or historic right to it."*

**Job 5:12**

*He thwarts the plans of the crafty, so that their hands achieve no success.*

**Job 6:13**

*Do I have any power to help myself, now that success has been driven from me?*

**Psalms 118:25**

*O LORD, save us; O LORD, grant us success.*

**Ecclesiastes 10:10**

*If the ax is dull and its edge unsharpened, more strength is needed but skill will bring success.*

**Daniel 11:14**

*"In those times many will rise against the king of the South. The violent men among your own people will rebel in fulfillment of the vision, but without success.*

## Prosper

**Genesis 24:40**

*But he said to me, 'The LORD, before whom I walk, will send His angel with you and prosper your way; and you shall take a wife for my son from my family and from my father's house. NKJV*

**Genesis 24:42**

*And this day I came to the well and said, 'O LORD God of my master Abraham, if you will now prosper the way in which I go, NKJV*

**Genesis 26:13**

*The man began to prosper, and continued prospering until he became very prosperous; NKJV*

**Genesis 39:3**

*And his master saw that the LORD was with him and that the LORD made all he did to prosper in his hand. NKJV*

**Genesis 39:23**

*The keeper of the prison did not look into anything that was under Joseph's authority, because the LORD was with him; and whatever he did, the LORD made it prosper. NKJV*

**Deuteronomy 28:29**

*And you shall grope at noonday, as a blind man gropes in darkness; you shall not prosper in your ways; you shall be only oppressed and plundered continually, and no one shall save you. NKJV*

**Deuteronomy 29:9**

*Therefore keep the words of this covenant, and do them, that you may prosper in all that you do. NKJV*

**Deuteronomy 30:5**

*Then the LORD your God will bring you to the land which your fathers possessed, and you shall possess it. He will prosper you and multiply you more than your fathers. NKJV*

**Joshua 1:7**

*Only be strong and very courageous, that you may observe to do according to all the law which Moses My servant commanded you; do not turn from it to the right hand or to the left, that you may prosper wherever you go. NKJV*

**Ruth 4:11**

*And all the people who were at the gate, and the elders, said, "We are witnesses. The LORD make the woman who is coming to your house like Rachel and Leah, the two who built the house of Israel; and may you prosper in Ephrathah and be famous in Bethlehem. NKJV*

**I Kings 2:3**

*And keep the charge of the LORD your God: to walk in His ways, to keep His statutes, His commandments, His judgments, and His testimonies, as it is written in the Law of Moses, that you may prosper in all that you do and wherever you turn; NKJV*

**I Kings 22:12**

*And all the prophets prophesied so, saying, "Go up to Ramoth Gilead and prosper, for the LORD will deliver it into the king's hand." NKJV*

**I Kings 22:15**

*Then he came to the king; and the king said to him, "Micaiah, shall we go to war against Ramoth Gilead, or shall we refrain?" And he answered him, "Go and prosper, for the LORD will deliver it into the hand of the king!" NKJV*

**1 Chronicles 22:11**

*Now, my son, may the LORD be with you; and may you prosper, and build the house of the LORD your God, as He has said to you. NKJV*

**1 Chronicles 22:13**

*Then you will prosper, if you take care to fulfill the statutes and judgments with which the LORD charged Moses concerning Israel. Be strong and of good courage; do not fear nor be dismayed. NKJV*

**2 Chronicles 13:12**

*Now look, God Himself is with us as our head, and His priests with sounding trumpets to sound the alarm against you. O children of Israel, do not fight against the LORD God of your fathers, for you shall not prosper!" NKJV*

**2 Chronicles 18:11**

*And all the prophets prophesied so, saying, "Go up to Ramoth Gilead and prosper, for the LORD will deliver it into the king's hand." NKJV*

**2 Chronicles 18:14**

*Then he came to the king; and the king said to him, "Micaiah, shall we go to war against Ramoth Gilead, or shall I refrain?" And he said, "Go and prosper, and they shall be delivered into your hand!" NKJV*

**2 Chronicles 20:20**

*So they rose early in the morning and went out into the Wilderness of Tekoa; and as they went out, Jehoshaphat stood and said, "Hear me, O Judah and you inhabitants of Jerusalem: Believe in the LORD your God, and you shall be established; believe His prophets, and you shall prosper." NKJV*

**2 Chronicles 24:20**

*Then the Spirit of God came upon Zechariah the son of Jehoiada the priest, who stood above the people, and said to them, "Thus says God: 'Why do you transgress the commandments of the LORD, so that you cannot prosper? Because you have forsaken the LORD, He also has forsaken you.' " NKJV*

**2 Chronicles 26:5**

*He sought God in the days of Zechariah, who had understanding in the visions of God; and as long as he sought the LORD, God made him prosper. NKJV*

**2 Chronicles 31:21**

*And every work which he began in the service of the house of God in law and in commandment, seeking his God, he did with all his heart and prospered. NASB*

**Nehemiah 1:11**

*O Lord, I pray, please let Your ear be attentive to the prayer of Your servant, and to the prayer of Your servants who desire to fear Your name; and let Your servant prosper this day, I pray, and grant him mercy in the sight of this man." For I was the king's cupbearer. NKJV*

**Nehemiah 2:20**

*So I answered them, and said to them, "The God of heaven Himself will prosper us; therefore we His servants will arise and build, but you have no heritage or right or memorial in Jerusalem." NKJV*

**Job 8:6**

*If you were pure and upright, surely now He would awake for you, and prosper your rightful dwelling place. NKJV*

**Job 12:6**

*6 The tents of robbers prosper, and those who provoke God are secure-- in what God provides by His hand. NKJV*

**Psalms 1:3**

*He shall be like a tree planted by the rivers of water, that brings forth its fruit in its season, whose leaf also shall not wither; and whatever he does shall prosper. NKJV*

**Psalms 122:6**

*Pray for the peace of Jerusalem: "May they prosper who love you. NKJV*

**Proverbs 3:10**

*Then your barns will be filled to overflowing, and your vats will brim over with new wine.*

**Proverbs 28:13**

*He who covers his sins will not prosper, but whoever confesses and forsakes them will have mercy. NKJV*

**Ecclesiastes 11:6**

*In the morning sow your seed, and in the evening do not withhold your hand; for you do not know which will prosper, either this or that, or whether both alike will be good. NKJV*

**Isaiah 48:15**

*I, even I, have spoken; yes, I have called him, I have brought him, and his way will prosper. NKJV*

**Isaiah 53:10**

*Yet it pleased the LORD to bruise Him; he has put Him to grief. When You make His soul an offering for sin, he shall see His seed, He shall prolong His days, and the pleasure of the LORD shall prosper in His hand. NKJV*

**Isaiah 54:17**

*No weapon formed against you shall prosper, and every tongue which rises against you in judgment you shall condemn. This is the heritage of the servants of the LORD, and their righteousness is from Me," says the LORD. NKJV*

**Isaiah 55:11**

*So shall My word be that goes forth from My mouth; it shall not return to Me void, but it shall accomplish what I please, and it shall prosper in the thing for which I sent it. NKJV*

**Jeremiah 2:37**

*Indeed you will go forth from him with your hands on your head; for the LORD has rejected your trusted allies, and you will not prosper by them. NKJV*

**Jeremiah 5:28**

*They have grown fat, they are sleek; yes, they surpass the deeds of the wicked; they do not plead the cause, the cause of the fatherless; yet they prosper, and the right of the needy they do not defend. NKJV*

**Jeremiah10:21**

*For the shepherds have become dull-hearted, and have not sought the LORD; therefore they shall not prosper, and all their flocks shall be scattered. NKJV*

**Jeremiah 12:1**

*Righteous are You, O LORD, when I plead with You; yet let me talk with You about Your judgments. Why does the way of the wicked prosper? Why are those happy who deal so treacherously? NKJV*

**Jeremiah 20:11**

*But the LORD is with me as a mighty, awesome One. Therefore my persecutors will stumble, and will not prevail. They will be greatly ashamed, for they will not prosper. Their everlasting confusion will never be forgotten. NKJV*

**Jeremiah 22:30**

*Thus says the LORD: 'Write this man down as childless, a man who shall not prosper in his days; for none of his descendants shall prosper, sitting on the throne of David, and ruling anymore in Judah.' NKJV*

**Jeremiah 23:5-6**

*Behold, the days are coming," says the LORD, "That I will raise to David a Branch of righteousness; a King shall reign and prosper, and execute judgment and righteousness in the earth. In His days Judah will be saved, and Israel will dwell safely; now this is His name by which He will be called: THE LORD OUR RIGHTEOUSNESS. NKJV*

**Lamentations 1:5**

*Her adversaries have become the master, her enemies prosper; for the LORD has afflicted her because of the multitude of her transgressions. Her children have gone into captivity before the enemy. NKJV*

**Ezekiel 17:15**

*'But he rebelled against him by sending his ambassadors to Egypt, that they might give him horses and many people. Will he prosper? Will he who does such things escape? Can he break a covenant and still be delivered? NKJV*

**Daniel 8:24**

*His power shall be mighty, but not by his own power; he shall destroy fearfully, and shall prosper and thrive; he shall destroy the mighty, and also the holy people. NKJV*

**Daniel 8:25**

*Through his cunning he shall cause deceit to prosper under his rule; and he shall exalt himself in his heart. He shall destroy many in their prosperity. He shall even rise against the Prince of princes; but he shall be broken without human means. NKJV*

**Daniel 11:27**

*Both these kings' hearts shall be bent on evil, and they shall speak lies at the same table; but it shall not prosper, for the end will still be at the appointed time. NKJV*

**Daniel 11:36**

*Then the king shall do according to his own will: he shall exalt and magnify himself above every god, shall speak blasphemies against the God of gods, and shall prosper till the wrath has been accomplished; for what has been determined shall be done. NKJV*

**1 Corinthians 16:2**

*On the first day of the week let each one of you lay something aside, storing up as he may prosper, that there be no collections when I come. NKJV*

**3 John 1:2**

*Beloved, I pray that you may prosper in all things and be in health, just as your soul prospers. NKJV*

## Prosperity

**Deuteronomy 23:5 -6**

*You shall not seek their peace nor their prosperity all your days forever. NIV*

**Deuteronomy 28:11**

*And the LORD will make you abound in prosperity, in the offspring of your body and in the offspring of your beast and in the produce of your ground, in the land which the LORD swore to your fathers to give you. NASB*

**Deuteronomy 28:12**

*The LORD will open the heavens, the storehouse of his bounty, to send rain on your land in season and to bless all the work of your hands. You will lend to many nations but will borrow from none."*

**1 Samuel 25:5-6**

*And thus you shall say to him who lives in prosperity: 'Peace be to you, peace to your house, and peace to all that you have! NIV*

**1 Kings 10:7**

*However I did not believe the words until I came and saw with my own eyes; and indeed the half was not told me.*

*Your wisdom and prosperity exceed the fame of which I heard. NIV*

**Ezra 9:12-13**

*Now therefore, do not give your daughters as wives for their sons, nor take their daughters to your sons; and never seek their peace or prosperity, that you may be strong and eat the good of the land, and leave it as an inheritance to your children forever.' NIV*

**Job 15:21**

*Dreadful sounds are in his ears; In prosperity the destroyer comes upon him. NIV*

**Job 21:16**

*Indeed their prosperity is not in their hand; the counsel of the wicked is far from me. NIV*

**Job 30:15**

*Terrors are turned upon me; They pursue my honor as the wind, and my prosperity has passed like a cloud. NIV*

**Job 36:11-12**

*If they obey and serve Him, They shall spend their days in prosperity, And their years in pleasures. But if they do not obey, They shall perish by the sword, And they shall die without knowledge. NIV*

**Psalms 25:13**

*He himself shall dwell in prosperity, And his descendants shall inherit the earth. NIV*

**Psalms 30:6-7**

*Now in my prosperity I said, "I shall never be moved." LORD, by Your favor You have made my mountain stand strong; You hid Your face, and I was troubled. NIV*

**Psalms 35:27**

*Let them shout for joy and be glad, Who favor my righteous cause; And let them say continually, "Let the LORD be magnified, Who has pleasure in the prosperity of His servant." NIV*

**Psalms 68:6**

*God sets the solitary in families; He brings out those who are bound into prosperity; But the rebellious dwell in a dry land. NIV*

**Psalms 73:3**

*For I was envious of the boastful, When I saw the prosperity of the wicked. NIV*

**Psalms 118:25**

*Save now, I pray, O LORD; O LORD, I pray, send now prosperity. NIV*

**Psalms 122:7**

*Peace be within your walls, Prosperity within your palaces." NIV*

**Ecclesiastes 7:14**

*In the day of prosperity be joyful, But in the day of adversity consider: Surely God has appointed the one as well as the other, So that man can find out nothing that will come after him. NIV*

**Jeremiah 22:21**

*I spoke to you in your prosperity, But you said, 'I will not hear.' This has been your manner from your youth, That you did not obey My voice. NIV*

**Jeremiah 33:9**

*Then it shall be to Me a name of joy, a praise, and an honor before all nations of the earth, who shall hear all the good that I do to them; they shall fear and tremble for all the goodness and all the prosperity that I provide for it.' NIV*

**Lamentations 3:17-18**

*You have moved my soul far from peace; I have forgotten prosperity. And I said, "My strength and my hope Have perished from the LORD." NIV*

**Daniel 4:27**

*Therefore, O king, let my advice be acceptable to you; break off your sins by being righteous, and your iniquities by showing mercy to the poor. Perhaps there may be a lengthening of your prosperity." NIV*

**Daniel 8:25**

*Through his cunning He shall cause deceit to prosper under his rule; And he shall exalt himself in his heart. He shall destroy many in their prosperity. He shall even rise against the Prince of princes; But he shall be broken without human means. NIV*

**Zechariah 1:17**

*Again proclaim, saying, 'Thus says the LORD of hosts: "My cities shall again spread out through prosperity; The LORD will again comfort Zion, And will again choose Jerusalem.' NIV*

**Acts 19:25**

*He called them together with the workers of similar occupation, and said: "Men, you know that we have our prosperity by this trade. NIV*

**Acts 24:2-4**

*And when he was called upon, Tertullus began his accusation, saying: "Seeing that through you we enjoy great peace, and prosperity is being brought to this nation by your foresight, we accept it always and in all places, most noble Felix, with all thankfulness. NIV*

**Luke 15:13**

*And not many days later, the younger son gathered everything together and went on a journey into a distant country, and there he squandered his estate with loose living. NASB*

**John 6:12**

*And when they were filled, He said to His disciples, "Gather up the leftover fragments that nothing may be lost." NASB*

## Prosperous

**Genesis 24:2**

*And the man, wondering at her, remained silent so as to know whether the LORD had made his journey prosperous or not. NKJV*

**Genesis 26:13**

*The man began to prosper, and continued prospering until he became very prosperous; NKJV*

**Genesis 30:4**

*Thus the man became exceedingly prosperous, and had large flocks, female and male servants, and camels and donkeys. NKJV*

**Joshua 1:8**

*This Book of the Law shall not depart from your mouth, but you shall meditate in it day and night, that you may observe to do according to all that is written in it. For then you will make your way prosperous, and then you will have good success. NKJV*

**Judges 18:5**

*So they said to him, "Please inquire of God, that we may know whether the journey on which we go will be prosperous." NKJV*

**Psalms 22:29**

*All the prosperous of the earth shall eat and worship; all those who go down to the dust shall bow before Him, even he who cannot keep himself alive. NKJV*

**Zechariah7:7**

*Should you not have obeyed the words which the LORD proclaimed through the former prophets when Jerusalem and the cities around it were inhabited and prosperous, and the South and the Lowland were inhabited? NKJV*

**Zechariah 8:12**

*For the seed shall be prosperous, The vine shall give its fruit, The ground shall give her increase, and the heavens shall give their dew - I will cause the remnant of this people To possess all these. NKJV*

# Summary

Psalms 139 says that God knew about you even before you were born. It states that you were fearfully and wonderfully made. In others words, you were created with "purpose." And according to verse 16, all of your days were ordained for you and written in God's book even before you took your first breath.

Romans 8:28 is one of the best-loved passages in the Bible. It says this. "We know that all things work together for good to them that love God, to them who are the called according to his purpose." God has a good and great purpose in mind for you. You can trust Him with your life.

God wants for you to be successful! Achieving personal success is always the result of a lot of planning, intense work, good habits and continual follow through. We are what we repeatedly do. Excellence is not an act but a habit. Success is a planned event and rarely happens without great personal effort.

**Philippians 4:13**

*I can do all things through Christ who strengthens me (NKJV).*

**Psalms 139:5-6**

*You hem me in-- behind and before; you have laid your hand upon me. Such knowledge is too wonderful for me, too lofty for me to attain. (NIV)*

**Romans 8:31**

> *What shall we then say to these things? If God be for us, who can be against us?" (KJV)*

God is on your side! He wants you to reach forward into your future and secure the destiny He has for your life!

# EndNotes


1. Page 166, The Principles and Power of Vision, Myles Munroe, 2003, Whitaker House
2. Page 29, Now Discover Your Strengths, Marcus Buckingham & Donald Clifton, 2001, The Free Press
3. The American Heritage® Dictionary of the English Language, Fourth Edition
4. Webster's Revised Unabridged Dictionary, © 1996, 1998 MICRA, Inc.
5. Sproul, Jr., R. C. Biblical Economics. Tennessee: Draught Horse Press, 2002, p.23.
6. Page 29, Business Buy The Bible by Wade B. Cook, 1997, Lighthouse Publishing Group, Inc.
7. Page 40, Today Matters, John C. Maxwell, 2004, Warner Faith
8. Page 85, Business Proverbs by Steve Marr, published in 2001 by Fleming H. Revel, A Division of Baker Book House.
9. Page 37, 21 Unbreakable Laws of Life, Max Anders, 1996, Thomas Nelson
10. Charles J. Givens, author of SuperSelf: Doubling Your Personal Effectiveness (Simon & Schuster)
11. Page 22, The Impossible is Possible by John Mason, Bethany House Publishers

# Source Material


21 Unbreakable Laws of Success, Max Anders, Thomas Nelson, 1996
A Christian Guide to Prosperity; Fries & Taylor, California: Communications Research, 1984
A Look At Stewardship, Word Aflame Publications, 2001
American Savings Education Council (http://www.asec.org)
Anointed For Business, Ed Silvoso, Regal, 2002
Avoiding Common Financial Mistakes, Ron Blue, Navpress, 1991
Baker Encyclopedia of the Bible; Walter Elwell, Michigan: Baker Book House, 1988
Becoming The Best, Barry Popplewell, England: Gower Publishing Company Limited, 1988
Business Proverbs, Steve Marr, Fleming H. Revell, 2001
Cheapskate Monthly, Mary Hunt
Commentary on the Old Testament; Keil-Delitzsch, Michigan: Eerdmans Publishing, 1986
Crown Financial Ministries, various publications
Customers As Partners, Chip Bell, Texas: Berrett-Koehler Publishers, 1994
Cut Your Bills in Half; Pennsylvania: Rodale Press, Inc., 1989
Debt-Free Living, Larry Burkett, Dimensions, 2001
Die Broke, Stephen M. Pollan & Mark Levine, HarperBusiness, 1997
Double Your Profits, Bob Fifer, Virginia: Lincoln Hall Press, 1993
Eerdmans' Handbook to the Bible, Michigan: William B. Eerdmans Publishing Company, 1987
Eight Steps to Seven Figures, Charles B. Carlson, Double Day, 2000
Everyday Life in Bible Times; Washington DC: National Geographic Society, 1967
Financial Dominion, Norvel Hayes, Harrison House, 1986
Financial Freedom, Larry Burkett, Moody Press, 1991
Financial Freedom, Patrick Clements, VMI Publishers, 2003
Financial Peace, Dave Ramsey, Viking Press, 2003
Financial Self-Defense; Charles Givens, New York: Simon And Schuster, 1990
Flood Stage, Oral Roberts, 1981
Generous Living, Ron Blue, Zondervan, 1997
Get It All Done, Tony and Robbie Fanning, New York:Pennsylvania: Chilton Book, 1979
Getting Out of Debt, Howard Dayton, Tyndale House, 1986

Getting Out of Debt, Mary Stephenson, Fact Sheet 436, University of Maryland Cooperative Extension Service, 1988
Giving and Tithing, Larry Burkett, Moody Press, 1991
God's Plan For Giving, John MacArthur, Jr., Moody Press, 1985
God's Will is Prosperity, Gloria Copeland, Harrison House, 1978
Great People of the Bible and How They Lived; New York: Reader's Digest, 1974
How Others Can Help You Get Out of Debt; Esther M. Maddux, Circular 759-3,
How To Make A Business Plan That Works, Henderson, North Island Sound Limited, 1989
How To Manage Your Money, Larry Burkett, Moody Press, 1999
How to Personally Profit From the Laws of Success, Sterling Sill, NIFP, Inc., 1978
How to Plan for Your Retirement; New York: Corrigan & Kaufman, Longmeadow Press, 1985
Is God Your Source?, Oral Roberts, 1992
It's Not Luck, Eliyahu Goldratt, Great Barrington, MA: The North River Press, 1994
Jesus CEO, Laurie Beth Jones, Hyperion, 1995
John Avanzini Answers Your Questions About Biblical Economics, Harrison House, 1992
Living on Less and Liking It More, Maxine Hancock, Chicago, Illinois: Moody Press, 1976
Making It Happen; Charles Conn, New Jersey: Fleming H. Revell Company, 1981
Master Your Money Or It Will Master You, Arlo E. Moehlenpah, Doing Good Ministries, 1999
Master Your Money; Ron Blue, Tennessee: Thomas Nelson, Inc. 1986
Miracle of Seed Faith, Oral Roberts, 1970
Mississippi State University Extension Service
Money, Possessions, and Eternity, Randy Alcorn, Tyndale House, 2003
More Than Enough, David Ramsey, Penguin Putnam Inc, 2002
Moving the Hand of God, John Avanzini, Harrison House, 1990
Multiplication, Tommy Barnett, Creation House, 1997
NebFacts, Nebraska Cooperative Extension
New York Post
One Up On Wall Street; New York: Peter Lynch, Simon And Schuster, 1989
Personal Finances, Larry Burkett, Moody Press, 1991
Portable MBA in Finance and Accounting; Livingstone, Canada: John Wiley & Sons, Inc., 1992
Principle-Centered Leadership, Stephen R. Covey, New York: Summit Books, 1991
Principles of Financial Management, Kolb & DeMong, Texas: Business Publications, Inc., 1988
Rapid Debt Reduction Strategies, John Avanzini, HIS Publishing, 1990
Real Wealth, Wade Cook, Arizona: Regency Books, 1985
See You At The Top, Zig Ziglar, Louisianna: Pelican Publishing Company, 1977

Seed-Faith Commentary on the Holy Bible, Oral Roberts, Pinoak Publications, 1975
Sharkproof, Harvey Mackay, New York: HarperCollins Publishers, 1993
Smart Money, Ken and Daria Dolan, New York: Random House, Inc., 1988
Strong's Concordance, Tennessee: Crusade Bible Publishers, Inc.,
Success by Design, Peter Hirsch, Bethany House, 2002
Success is the Quality of your Journey, Jennifer James, New York: Newmarket Press, 1983
Swim with the Sharks Without Being Eaten Alive, Harvey Mackay, William Morrow , 1988
The Almighty and the Dollar; Jim McKeever, Oregon: Omega Publications, 1981
The Challenge, Robert Allen, New York: Simon And Schuster, 1987
The Family Financial Workbook, Larry Burkett, Moody Press, 2002
The Management Methods of Jesus, Bob Briner, Thomas Nelson, 1996
The Millionaire Next Door, Thomas Stanley & William Danko, Pocket Books, 1996
The Money Book for Kids, Nancy Burgeson, Troll Associates,1992
The Money Book for King's Kids; Harold E. Hill, New Jersey: Fleming H. Revell Company, 1984
The Seven Habits of Highly Effective People, Stephen Covey, New York: Simon And Schuster, 1989
The Wealthy Barber, David Chilton, California: Prima Publishing, 1991
Theological Wordbook of the Old Testament, Chicago, Illinois: Moody Press, 1981
Treasury of Courage and Confidence, Norman Vincent Peale, New York: Doubleday & Co., 1970
True Prosperity, Dick Iverson, Bible Temple Publishing, 1993
Trust God For Your Finances, Jack Hartman, Lamplight Publications, 1983
University of Georgia Cooperative Extension Service, 1985
Virginia Cooperative Extension
Webster's Unabridged Dictionary, Dorset & Baber, 1983
What Is an Entrepreneur; David Robinson, MA: Kogan Page Limited, 1990
Word Meanings in the New Testament, Ralph Earle, Michigan: Baker Book House, 1986
Word Pictures in the New Testament; Robertson, Michigan: Baker Book House, 1930
Word Studies in the New Testament; Vincent, New York: Charles Scribner's Sons, 1914
Worth
You Can Be Financially Free, George Fooshee, Jr., 1976, Fleming H. Revell Company.
Your Key to God's Bank, Rex Humbard, 1977
Your Money Counts, Howard, Dayton, Tyndale House, 1997
Your Money Management, MaryAnn Paynter, Circular 1271, University of Illinois Cooperative Extension Service, 1987.
Your Money Matters, Malcolm MacGregor, Bethany Fellowship, Inc., 1977
Your Road to Recovery, Oral Roberts, Oliver Nelson, 1986

# Comments On Sources

Over the years I have collected bits and pieces of interesting material, written notes on sermons I've heard, jotted down comments on financial articles I've read, and gathered a lot of great information. It is unfortunate that I didn't record the sources of all of these notes in my earlier years. I gratefully extend my appreciation to the many writers, authors, teachers and pastors from whose articles and sermons I have gleaned much insight.

*Rich Brott*

# Online Resources

American Savings Education Council (http://www.asec.org)
Bloomberg.com (http://www.bloomberg.com)
Bureau of the Public Debt Online (http://www.publicdebt.treas.gov)
BusinessWeek (http://www.businessweek.com)
Charles Schwab & Co., Inc. (http://www.schwab.com)
Consumer Federation of America (http://www.consumerfed.org)
Debt Advice.org (http://www.debtadvice.org)
Federal Reserve System (http://www.federalreserve.gov)
Fidelity Investments (http://www.fidelity.com)
Financial Planning Association (http://www.fpanet.org)
Forbes (www.forbes.com)
Fortune Magazine (http://www.fortune.com)
Generous Giving (http://www.generousgiving.org/)
Investing for Your Future (http://www.investing.rutgers.edu)
Kiplinger Magazine (http://www.kiplinger.com/)
Money Magazine (http://money.cnn.com)
MorningStar (http://www.morningstar.com)
MSN Money (http://moneycentral.msn.com)
Muriel Siebert (http://www.siebertnet.com)
National Center on Education and the Economy (http://www.ncee.org)
National Foundation for Credit Counseling (http://www.nfcc.org)
Quicken (http://www.quicken.com)
Smart Money (http://www.smartmoney.com)
Social Security Online (http://www.ssa.gov)
Standard & Poor's (http://www2.standardandpoors.com)
The Dollar Stretcher, Gary Foreman, (http://www.stretcher.com)
The Vanguard Group (http://flagship.vanguard.com)
U.S. Securities and Exchange Commission (http://www.sec.gov)
Yahoo! Finance (http://finance.yahoo.com)

# Magazine Resources

Business Week
Consumer Reports
Forbes
Kiplinger's Personal Finance
Money
Smart Money
US News and World Report

# Newspaper Resources

Barrons
Investors Business Daily
USA Today
Wall Street Journal
Washington Times

# Additional Resources by Rich Brott

## 15 Biblical Responsibilities Leading to Financial Wisdom

*Accepting Personal Accountability*

By Rich Brott

6" x 9", 120 pages
ISBN 1-60185-010-7
ISBN (EAN) 978-1-60185-010-2

***Order online at:***

www.amazon.com
www.barnesandnoble.com
www.booksamillion.com
www.citychristianpublishing.com
www.bordersstores.com

**www.AbcBookPublishing.com**

# Additional Resources by Rich Brott

## Biblical Principles for Achieving Personal Success

*8 Critical Insights You Must Discover!*

By Rich Brott

6" x 9", 248 pages
ISBN 1-60185-013-1
ISBN (EAN) 978-1-60185-013-3

***Order online at:***

www.amazon.com
www.barnesandnoble.com
www.booksamillion.com
www.citychristianpublishing.com
www.bordersstores.com

**www.AbcBookPublishing.com**

# Additional Resources by Rich Brott

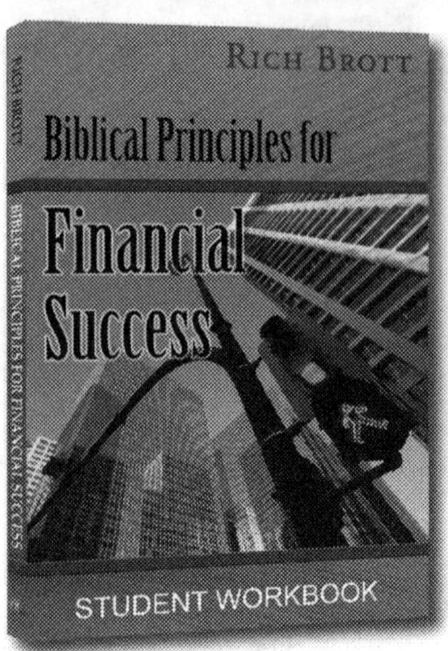


## Biblical Principles for Financial Success

*Student Workbook*

By Rich Brott

7.5" x 9.25", 228 pages
ISBN 1-60185-016-6
ISBN (EAN) 978-1-60185-016-4

***Order online at:***

www.amazon.com
www.barnesandnoble.com
www.booksamillion.com
www.citychristianpublishing.com
www.bordersstores.com

**www.AbcBookPublishing.com**

# Additional Resources by Rich Brott

## Biblical Principles for Building a Successful Business

*A Practical Guide to Assessing, Evaluating, and Growing a Successful Cutting-Edge Enterprise in Today's Business Environment*

By Rich Brott & Frank Damazio

7.5" x 10", 477 pages
ISBN 1-59383-027-0
ISBN (EAN) 978-1-59383-027-4

***Order online at:***

www.amazon.com
www.barnesandnoble.com
www.booksamillion.com
www.citychristianpublishing.com
www.bordersstores.com

**www.AbcBookPublishing.com**